Praise for
Generation NGO

"*Generation NGO* is essential prior-to-departure reading as more and more young people elect to volunteer overseas. This book is sure to inspire as well as to trouble its readers."
> —**Sally Humphries**, Director, International Development Studies, University of Guelph

"Young Canadians set forth into the developing world to try to bring about positive change. But while their objectives are not always achieved—or even achievable—their tales show how they themselves are often more transformed in the process than the wide world they seek to help."
> —**Alexandre Trudeau**, director of *Refuge, A Film About Darfur*

"In these astute and beautifully written personal essays, the authors critically engage with broad issues of development and social justice and interrogate their own role on the global stage. They leave us with much to ponder about the exhilaration, commitment, and ethical ambiguities that characterize the experience of Generation NGO."
> —**Jacqueline Solway**, Professor, International Development Studies and Anthropology, Trent University, and former Director of the Trent in Ghana program

"These personal accounts of development theory, taken to and tested in the field, provide excellent insights into what can go wrong, what can go right, what surprises can come up, and what can be painfully, predictably, constant."
> —**Thomas Meredith**, Associate Professor, Department of Geography, McGill University, and Director, Canadian Field Studies in Africa

Generation NGO

Edited by
Alisha Nicole Apale and Valerie Stam

BETWEEN THE LINES

Toronto

Generation NGO

First published in 2011 by
Between the Lines
401 Richmond Street West, Studio 277
Toronto, Ontario M5V 3A8
Canada
1-800-718-7201
www.btlbooks.com

Library and Archives Canada Cataloguing in Publication

Generation NGO / Alisha Nicole Apale & Valerie Stam, eds.

ISBN 978-1-897071-75-5

1. Young volunteers—Developing countries. 2. Young adults—Political activity—Canada. 3. Young adults—Canada—Attitudes. 4. Economic assistance, Canadian—Developing countries. 5. Technical assistance, Canadian—Developing countries. I. Apale, Alisha Nicole II. Stam, Valerie

HN49 V64.G45 2011   361.7′63   C2011-900989-7

Cover and text design by David Vereschagin/Quadrat Communications
Front cover photo by Iñigo Quintanilla/iStockphoto.com
Back cover photo by Alisha Nicole Apale taken in Tamil Nadu, India, 2007.
Printed in Canada

MIX
Paper from
responsible sources
FSC® C004071

Between the Lines gratefully acknowledges assistance for its publishing activities from the Canada Council for the Arts, the Ontario Arts Council, the Government of Ontario through the Ontario Book Publishers Tax Credit program and through the Ontario Book Initiative, and the Government of Canada through the Canada Book Fund.

Canada Council
for the Arts

Conseil des Arts
du Canada

ONTARIO ARTS COUNCIL
CONSEIL DES ARTS DE L'ONTARIO

Contents

Preface

The idea for this book was born during a hike in the woods, a catch-up visit with friends between bouts of travelling. As we hiked, we talked about our recent travels in Thailand and Senegal, the challenges we had faced, and the people we had met. A large number of our friends were having similar conversations, sometimes via long, often amusing email missives sent to friends and family back home while they were working overseas. While entertaining, these conversations also acted as a sounding board on some of the ethical issues faced in development work. They raised questions about what it was like to weave in and out of life abroad and back home.

It seemed that our generation had something valuable to share, some insights about the world of international development from the perspective of its freshest faces. We realized that this set of experiences had yet to be explored. It was these observations that inspired the creation of this book, an attempt to capture our journeys—full of emotion, expectation, and questioning—in a more permanent fashion than just sending them off into cyberspace.

Generation NGO is a trailhead of sorts. We see the ethical dilemmas and reflections that accompany all development workers, no matter their years of experience, from the perspective of beginners. This book is much more about questions than it is about answers. Our inconsistent use of terms such as "Third World," "First World," "underdeveloped," and "low income" highlights the troubled terminology of the sector. It is a language filled with classist, sexist, and racist hierarchy and old colonial tropes, a lexicon burdened by a history of foreign occupation, impunity, and cultural dispossession.

The process of writing enabled us to distil our first experiences with inequality and poverty, thus formulating views on power and privilege, stereotypes, identity, social location, prejudice, and injustice, among other topics. We wanted to capture these first impressions before they were lost to the dusty corners of memory, overinterpreted and emotionally flattened. In a more personal sense, our stories illustrate the continual negotiation involved in positioning and conducting ourselves in a morally and ethically charged profession. For example, what do we do when faced with bribery and corruption? How do we respond to the sanctioned prejudice that thrives in a post-9/11 world obsessed with terrorism and security concerns? How do we react to pay inequities between international and national staff, or attitudes of deference toward white foreigners? How do we deal with the riskier aspects of development work—larger-than-life experiences like kidnappings, human trafficking, or arms smuggling—without sounding like cowboys?

These stories are only a beginning. They present the shaky first formulations of a response to moral incertitude and ethical dilemmas that we continue to process long after returning from the field and years into our careers. *Generation NGO* does not offer answers; rather, it is a glimpse into the journey we begin, sometimes unwittingly, when we touch down in foreign land.

At times these stories betray naïveté. Ultimately, after a relatively short stint in the field, most of us seem to understand far more about our own biases than we do about how individuals and communities experience and contribute to their own development. This introspection is the crux of our journey, the key to turning questions into answers as we move ahead.

In soliciting contributions for *Generation NGO*, we wanted to represent the diversity of experiences we have as young professionals in the international development sector. Although we have tried to reflect an accurate cross-section of people engaged in this work, most of our writers are female. This is unsurprising: as in the other helping professions, such as nursing or social work, an undergraduate class in international development tends to be disproportionately populated by women. Likewise, the majority of our writers are white Canadians of European descent. As with many young professionals in the field, each of our contributors is highly educated, with at least one postsecondary degree. All are middle or upper class. Similarly, though we tried to reflect experiences from different parts of the globe, the African continent dominates our contributors' experiences. This is indicative of Canadian government overseas development aid priorities until recently.

The title came much later. Suggested by a friend's father, perhaps it seems at first a misnomer. But while not all people of this generation travel or have worked for a non-governmental organization (NGO) in the developing world, we realized that many of our friends had, and their friends, and their friends' friends. Their experiences form an important discourse within a generation of youth; they reflect the perspectives, ideals, and visions of a generation of Canadians who are increasingly active and engaged in global issues. Many are eagerly poised to contribute—in smaller and even larger ways—to international development and the Canadian national politics that, for better or worse, shape this field.

As we journey, time and again we find that when it comes to development practice, everything is far more nuanced than expected. The notion of "doing good" can be impossibly complicated. Often forgotten in the hustle and bustle of trying to "save the world," the fundamental questions addressed in *Generation NGO* are too easily sidelined by hurried project deadlines and competing interests. None of us claim to have arrived at a definitive answer to these questions, but we are aware of the challenging journey we have begun. This book is one response among many to the myriad conversations about the relevance and promise, validity and impact of the broader development industry. In writing *Generation NGO*, we aspire to share honestly with others the questions and observations that arise from our early professional experiences in the world of international development work. These are our stories.[1]

Generation NGO exists because of all those who so generously shared their time, their homes, their families, and their lives with us when we were so far from home. Without each of you, our stories would not be what they are. Words are a paltry expression of our thanks, but we say them nonetheless. Thank you.

On hearing about the idea for this book, Stephen Strauss, the 'life-time editor' of one of our contributors, Simon Strauss, pronounced it *Generation NGO*.

A big thank you to Richard Swift and Camilla Blakeley for their insightful and meticulous editing. We also give our warmest thanks to the team at Between the Lines for believing in this project.

Finally, to the eight contributors who stuck with us through many years and many emails, thank you for your confidence and trust and for your commitment to helping us tell another side of the development story.

---

1 In order to protect identity and privacy, we have changed the names of some of the people in our stories.

Introduction
Contexts and Consequences

Babies with bloated bellies. Farmers staring pensively at the sky, longing for rain. Crowded refugee camps where hope dies. Impassioned appeals for donations. Mosquito nets. Bono.

For most Canadians, this is a common picture of overseas development aid. Many good stories have been written about Canadian aid dollars hard at work around the world, alleviating poverty, improving access to health and education, promoting peace and good governance. But how does Canadian foreign policy influence development projects? How does it reflect on Canadians working in the field in the eyes of local people? Canadian development workers quickly come to realize that there are many sides to the complex story of international development.

There is an innocence to Canadian popular understanding of the poverty and inequality that shape the global South. It is an innocence that assumes good, even charitable, intentions by officialdom and tends to fall into easy stereotypes about problems and remedies. When these simplistic remedies fall short or prove limited, clichés about corruption, overpopulation, or cultures of poverty soon follow, offered with a shrug of the shoulders. Even worse, these notions descend into a complacency tinged with racism. This attitude also provides fertile ground for a range of cynical self-interest, from mining companies to celebrities who claim to be "just trying to help."

But innocence is rarely entirely innocent, as the ten stories that follow reveal in different ways and in different places. First and foremost, the stories each convey the dawning realization that good intentions can never be assumed, and that power relations are embedded in ways of seeing, understanding, and doing. They describe the huge but essential challenge of grappling with complexity in a world badly rent by the uneven distribution of wealth and power.

Context is crucial to understanding the layers of truth, belief, perception, and experience that craft life. The context of life in an urban slum. The context of tight-knit rural villages. The context of comfortable, middle-class lives in Canada. The context of another culture and language and how it shapes psychology and understanding. The context of history, from which we inherit perceptions of each other and of value. The context of an international system that polarizes wealth and power. It is with these overlapping contexts and their interaction that the writers of *Generation NGO* grapple as they endeavour to make a difference.

THE INTERNATIONAL CONTEXT

Development is a highly ambiguous term, meaning very different things to different people. The development industry as it is known today began after the Second World War. In 1944 at Bretton Woods, the International Monetary Fund (IMF) and the World Bank were created to get Europe's war-stricken economy going again. The success of these institutions in Europe incited world leaders to try similar economic injections into the newly minted postcolonial states of the global South. Through the eyes of modernization theorists, development was seen as a simple matter of moving the Third World through the same process of modernization that had occurred in the First World via the Industrial Revolution.

Through the 1950s and 1960s, the IMF and the World Bank underwrote large infrastructure projects and channelled cash in the form of loans into low-income countries. At the same time, aid was being used to win hearts, minds, and states in the Cold War. Canada's aid program started with $25 million for South and Southeast Asia, targeting impoverished communities that were thought to be communist "breeding grounds."[1] Our aid efforts extended from the Caribbean in the late 1950s to Africa in the 1960s and Latin America in the 1970s. The Canadian International Development Agency (CIDA)—responsible for managing Canada's aid monies and partnerships—was established in 1968. In the same year, Prime Minister Pierre Elliott Trudeau, known for his interest in international development, took office. By the end of the 1960s, dependency theory had emerged to challenge the orthodox notion of development, which held that stimulus spending (particularly for resource extraction) could kick-start an economy and achieve higher, sustained rates of growth. Dependency theorists maintained that wealthy nations were being enriched by extracting resources from underdeveloped but resource-rich countries without providing fair compensation.

By the mid-1970s, the large loans that had been pumped into low-income countries had done little to improve the lives of the poor but had precipitated a debt crisis that undermined public finance throughout the global South. The Bretton Woods institutions implemented Structural Adjustment Programs (SAPs) throughout the 1970s and 1980s to ensure that debt obligations were met. These cut civil service bureaucracies and spending on social programs in an effort to trim the budget and decrease the debt load of low-income countries. Rising commodity and food prices, fuelled by increasing oil prices, led to widespread discontent with the IMF and the World Bank. Conventional, market-based development economics were increasingly called into question by the poor and their advocates. Those opposed to SAPs began promoting a grassroots, participatory alternative to conventional development, inspired in part by Paolo Freire's theories of popular education and critical pedagogy in Latin America.[2] People in many parts of the world began to take an interest in the power of social movements and civil society. This was a period of substantial growth in NGOs and volunteerism, spurred by an increase in the desire of people around the world (including Canadians, many of them young) to make common cause with the billions excluded from the global economy.

Now, in the early twenty-first century, development theory continues to focus on poverty alleviation by creating global consensus on initiatives laid out in the Millennium Development Goals (MDGs) signed by member countries of the United Nations in 2000. The MDGs aim to halve poverty by 2015, yet for the most part they do not address the systemic imbalance of power and capital and its historical causes. They fail to challenge rich countries to take their share of responsibility for the current global system, including systematic exploitation of natural resources, outsourcing of low-wage manufacturing to countries with inadequate salaries and poor human rights records, and the subjugation of farmers and food producers to the interests of big corporations. Many action items stemming from the MDGs oblige Third World countries to do all the heavy lifting, leaving First World countries to act merely as watchdogs. Human development theory emerged as a more inclusive and holistic approach from a synthesis of feminist, environmental, and welfare economics and sustainable development in the late 1990s, but some of its central ideas were not incorporated into the MDGs. The most notable human development proponent, Nobel prize winner Amartya Sen puts forward the notion of development as freedom, namely, the right to choose alternative ways of thinking and being, the value of individual freedom as a social good, and the importance of public policy in creating conditions for healthy discussion as a basis for shaping individual values.[3]

On September 11, 2001, the World Trade Center towers fell, ushering in new security considerations and a shift in focus from issues of good governance and corruption to fragile and failed states. Security is now a buzzword in international development. It is seen as a prerequisite to the success of any of the MDGs, from universal education to gender equality. Unfortunately, security is seen largely as a matter for the police and military. Other forms of security, like social security or food security, have fallen well down the development agenda. Aid dollars are being redirected for military purposes. Add to this the popularity of a market-driven, neoliberal approach to economics and associated spending cuts for social welfare, health, and education, and it is easy to see how official circles are drifting ever further away from human-centred approaches to development. But this grassroots alternative is still very much the starting point for the writers of *Generation NGO* as they begin to compare the story of development they have been told with what they actually see in the field.

The tensions between idealistic visions and pragmatic realities are evident in the stories told in this book. The writers have diverse motivations for working overseas. But once abroad, they quickly cease to be independent and unbiased development practitioners. As Canadian citizens, they are actors in the larger narrative of the international development industry. They witness the costs of development. They encounter deeply disruptive and destabilizing processes such as urbanization or advocacy for women's rights, which create tensions within families, communities, and entire states. Development is about change and, often, this change is not organic or self-driven. Instead, it takes a top-down approach. Conventional international development is largely externally driven, operating within the policies, and thus the interests, of the global North. Dissatisfied with simplistic remedies, the writers of *Generation NGO* are learning to situate themselves in this development minefield.

A SHIFTING CANADIAN CONTEXT

Since 2005, Canada has committed approximately 0.3 per cent of its gross national income (GNI) to development aid annually, giving just over $4 billion in 2009.[4] This money is used for a bewildering number of purposes: building health clinics, training foreign police, digging wells, financing high-tech labs to genetically engineer plant seeds, and starting the careers of many recent graduates through CIDA youth internships. What has it all accomplished?

Canadians have a cherished self-image as international humanitarians and peacekeepers, and our country has had an international presence since the 1950s. Yet most of us have little sense of how our tax dollars are used overseas or how our aid policy has followed shifts in foreign policy and changing notions of self-interest. Despite our reluctance to give up our international nice guy image, our reputation overseas is changing in favour of "hard power," an approach that is thought to better serve the national interest.

Four billion dollars per year may seem like a lot of money, but unfortunately it does not translate into much on the ground. It is also less of our GNI than we used to give; in 1986–87, we were giving almost 0.5 per cent to international aid.[5] It is shocking to consider that former prime minister Lester B. Pearson was already calling for a commitment of 0.7 per cent of GDP in 1968, a pledge we have never fulfilled. Only five donor countries (Netherlands, Luxembourg, Denmark, Sweden, and Norway) have ever met or exceeded this UN target.[6] Another eleven European countries have made firm commitments to reach 0.7 per cent by 2015 as part of the MDGs. Canada is one of the six remaining countries, the others being Australia, Japan, New Zealand, Switzerland, and the United States, that have not set a clear timeframe on increasing their ODA assistance to 0.7 per cent of GNI.[7] This figure has now been the avowed target for over four decades. Yet by 2010, no G8 country (the G8, comprising the eight most wealthy and influential countries in the world, acts as the main economic council of rich nations) had come close to giving that much or even to meeting its self-imposed target for ODA.[8]

The figure of $4 billion is even more misleading when it becomes clear that much of our aid money actually stays in Canada in the form of tied aid. According to the United Nations World Food Programme, in 2004 approximately 75 per cent of all food aid was tied; it came from donors' surplus stocks at home and was shipped as in-kind contributions to fulfil aid commitments.[9] Tied aid is not limited to emergencies; 50 per cent of all Canadian aid to underdeveloped countries is tied.[10] While Canada has slowly been untying its aid since 2000, as of 2007 we were still one of the worst offenders. Some of our peers, like the United Kingdom, have completely untied all aid.[11]

In 2007, a Senate Committee report was released castigating Canadian aid for forty years of failure in sub-Saharan Africa.[12] The report failed to spur the government into action, and the Canadian public still knows little about its government's values and priorities for international development. This leaves CIDA, in particular, directionless and susceptible to unpredictable shifts in directives as the government reacts to different policy issues. CIDA's disorientation is compounded by its frequent change in senior staff. It has had six ministers over the past ten years.[13] According to a report from the Office of the Auditor General of Canada, such regular changes to priorities and personnel "ha[ve] confused CIDA staff, recipient governments, and other donors, effectively undermining the agency's long-term predictability."[14] Overseas partners have experienced an increase in bureaucracy and waiting times for official responses and disbursement of funds. It is ironic that the very inability of the government to articulate clear direction for CIDA has made the agency vulnerable to internal government scrutiny and criticism.

Canada's inaction in the development arena is even more telling when compared to the amount of our GNI spent on military and defence. The military budget was more than $21 billion in 2008 (1.3 per cent of GDP), rising to $22 billion in 2009, making Canada the fifteenth largest military spender globally.[15] For a country that cherishes its humanitarian reputation, this military spending seems grossly disproportionate to the $4 billion spent annually on aid.

The shrinking Canadian commitment to international aid is a question not just of the quantity but also of the type of aid delivered. Though it began under the Liberal administration, Canada's role in the militarization of international aid has become entrenched on the Conservative government's watch. Canada has reoriented its foreign policy to a '3D' approach, marrying defence, diplomacy, and development. This shift is supposed to be a better way of coordinating actions in conflict zones such as Afghanistan. While appealing to bureaucratic efficiency, in reality the move blurs the lines between Canada's development work, foreign interests, and military operations. For example, the Canadian military is a key player in a now eight-year-long war in Afghanistan, while the government simultaneously supports

humanitarian activities in the country.[16] This role has Canada playing double agent: holding a gun in one hand and polio vaccines in the
other. Similarly, CIDA's $5 million funding of the Mirwais Hospital in
Kandahar may be seen as an attempt to legitimize, or soften, Canada's
military presence.[17] Integrating defence, foreign affairs, and development means that humanitarian activities serve non-humanitarian
interests and undermines safe, sustainable development projects
that aim to truly address the needs and interests articulated by local
communities.[18] The startling, and increasingly common, image of aid
workers wearing flak jackets and guarded by Canadian soldiers calls
into question the impartiality and neutrality of aid.

In 2007, Afghanistan consumed 8.5 per cent of all Canadian official development assistance (ODA). Now the "largest recipient of Canadian aid and military forces," Afghanistan is described as an opportunistic "laboratory" setting for experimentation with the 3D approach.[19]
This new orientation is a sharp contrast to 1956, when then minister
of external affairs Lester B. Pearson proposed the first UN peacekeeping mission in the Suez Canal. Pearson went on to receive the Nobel
Peace Prize for his innovative thinking and long-term commitment
to peace, which started a long history of blue-bereted peacekeepers,
often touted as a Canadian tradition. But our commitment to peacekeeping is steadily declining. In 2006, Canada was ranked fifty-fifth
out of 108 troop-contributing countries, with a total contribution of
just 126 military observers, UN police, and troops to UN peacekeeping missions.[20] Moreover, Canada contributed only 3.0 per cent of the
2006 assessed contributions to the UN peacekeeping budget of nearly
$5 billion.[21] Compare this to Canada's commitment as the sixth largest
contributor to the civil and military budgets of NATO, the North Atlantic Treaty Organization, an arguably non-pacifist organization with the
aim of protecting the interests of the global North.[22]

By combining development dollars with those of diplomacy and
defence, Canada can also use humanitarian work to deflect criticism
from its ideological and economic interests overseas. According to one
reporter at the *Globe and Mail*, "Canada's foreign aid seems to have

become an instrument of its trade policy."[23] Haiti is a good example of how development policy is used to support Canada's foreign and economic interests. Though it seems altruistic, Canada's historical involvement in Haiti has also been one of self-interest, undertaken in response to the unspoken expectation of other world powers that Canada pull its weight in "making an example" of popular democracies that are attempting to improve the life of the poor and also as a way to defend and expand the interests of Canadian corporations and capitalism abroad.[24] Canada's involvement in Haiti sends a clear message to the global South that countries should keep wages low and embrace free trade so that foreign companies can benefit from cheap labour, easy access to markets, and favourable legislation that serves the interests of corporations, not citizens. For example, Canadian companies have benefited from both the 2004 coup and the 2010 post-earthquake reconstruction. After the coup, Canada was instrumental in helping to devise, finance, implement, and legitimize the Interim Cooperation Framework that reversed many of the pro-poor economic achievements of the democratically elected governments of Presidents Jean-Bertrand Aristide and René Preval.[25] For instance, some Canadian apparel companies moved production to Haiti shortly after the coup to take advantage of the low wages guaranteed by the overthrow of Aristide, whose government had almost doubled the Haitian minimum wage a year earlier.[26] In addition, after the 2010 earthquake Canada became one of the ten foreign members of the Interim Haiti Recovery Commission (commonly known by its French acronym, CIRH), which has control over the finances and administration of Haiti during its reconstruction.[27] The Canadian position on the CIRH was secured through its donation of $100 million for two consecutive years to Haiti. The CIRH has been designed in such a way that it effectively cedes Haiti's autonomy to those with large sums of aid money.[28] This allows Canada to mould Haitian policy in ways that benefit Canadian economic interests. Canadian companies stand to gain from disaster capitalism following the earthquake, as preference for security and reconstruction contracts is being given to foreign bodies instead of local companies, which would, by extension, benefit the local economy.[29] For example, Canada is now taking the lead in providing security during the reconstruction and has allocated $9.5 million for the development of new headquarters for Haiti's national police force.[30] This concession of democratic control to states with big development dollars is emblematic of our times. Aid money is less about supporting sustainable development and more about opportunism. In the end, aid is not about human development. It boils down to power.

That benevolence and commercial interest regularly go hand in hand is a centuries-old narrative. When it comes to Canada's role in Africa's mining sector, however, benevolence is a thin veil indeed. Canadian companies eagerly invest in gas, oil, metal, and mineral resources.[31] The Toronto Stock Exchange is now the largest financial market in the African mining sector, with $21 billion in assets concentrated in thirty-three countries.[32] Yet while we are now one of the biggest players, Canada is not leading the way toward corporate social responsibility or other accountability measures.[33] Exploiting the environment and the workforce, Canadian neocolonial mining practices give rise to corruption, unstable employment, pervasive poverty, environmental degradation, and ill health around mining districts.[34] These practices run in sharp contrast to—and often to the detriment of—the overseas reputation Canadians pride themselves on and undermine many initiatives taken up by NGOs. It is worth questioning to what extent the convergence of the policy interests of our government, national defence system, and commercial industries will be allowed to take precedence over sustainable, human-centred forms of development.

Currently, the trajectory of Canada's ODA does not look promising. Despite a verbal commitment to the African continent, in 2009 the administration of Stephen Harper narrowed its approach to international development by shortening the already limited list of African countries receiving assistance from Canada. In Malawi, for example, multiyear development projects have ended mid-cycle and an entire embassy, only recently established, was shut down overnight.[35] At the same time, middle-income countries in South America and Eastern

Europe have been prioritized as aid recipients.[36] One part of the story that development practitioners, reporters, and the general public has been told is that this shift is beneficial for greater aid effectiveness, meaning that in addition to demonstrated need, the recipient country must *also* have the capacity to use aid productively *and* hold development priorities that are aligned with Canada's foreign policy.[37] Not mentioned is how this shift in focus will benefit Canada, and particularly its economic interests, as it targets more middle-income countries for development aid. Is Canada's development agenda intended to furnish some quick "wins"? Is the hope that easy successes will distract from our commercial self-interest, the militarization of our overseas presence, the erosion of our peacekeeping reputation, and our penchant for tied aid? The writers of *Generation NGO* are part of an increasingly reflective and critical group of development practitioners questioning the impact of Canadian development assistance on the ground.

GENERATION NGO AT HOME

While there is a mind-boggling diversity of approaches in the world of development organizations, the fact that they *are* non-governmental gives them a degree of leeway in their actions, even though these may run counter to government policy. Although this freedom can raise issues of accountability for their own work, it also allows NGOs to analyze government aid policies and advocate for more effective and accountable ones.

For all its faults, CIDA has a long history of funding NGOs that differ in ideology and practice from government policy. However, despite the arm's length relationship with government that NGOs have historically enjoyed, their funding has become increasingly subject to the interests and priorities of the government. For example, in early 2010, Harper and the Conservative Party came under fire for separating abortion from the G8 maternal and child health initiative.[38] This provoked a deeply polarized abortion debate that effectively politicized the initiative and distracted from other core issues of women's sexual and reproductive health. The Conservatives ended up promoting a health policy shaped by ideology rather than by a pragmatic concern for maternal health, putting women's health organizations that depend on CIDA funding in an impossible position. Overseas agencies providing abortion services as part of their women's health programs risk losing their Canadian funding.[39] According to Action Canada for Population and Development (ACPD) and its partners, "in order to receive funding from Canada, groups will have to separate their programs, creating costly administrative headaches and barriers. Further, groups who refuse to be complicit in the unnecessary deaths of women who have [back alley] abortions may decide to forfeit Canadian funding entirely, thereby reducing or even eliminating their ability to provide other basic healthcare."[40] While Canada was applauded for making maternal and child health the theme of the 2010 G8 summit, its reputation as a champion of women's health has been stained.

During its time in office, the Harper administration has systematically eliminated or reduced support for NGO partners that were plainly antithetical to a neoconservative agenda. In the process, the capacity of the NGO community to hold the government accountable has become increasingly limited. NGOs that concentrate on issues such as human and women's rights, those with a social justice orientation, or those that support social change have been systematically defunded. The government's technique is to sit, indefinitely, on a decision to renew funding, leaving organizations to fend for themselves when their CIDA-funded budgets run out. More worrisome is that this tactic has also affected the Canadian Council for International Co-operation (CCIC), the umbrella organization of the entire NGO community.[41] Restricting the capacity of CCIC is a way of limiting public debate on development assistance and reducing the coherence of the NGO community as a whole, particularly its ability to ensure that Canadian overseas aid priorities and policies are accountable to the Canadian public and recipient countries.

For Canadian NGOs operating at home, the politicization of funding disbursements also has far-reaching implications. The freedom to choose alternative ways of thinking and understanding and to create conditions for diverse and healthy public debate on issues of government policy is being curtailed. Long-standing organizations such as Kairos, an ecumenical social justice organization, and Alternatives, a Quebec NGO with a social justice mandate, have not had their CIDA funding renewed due to their critiques of Canadian involvement in Afghanistan and the Middle East.[42] Rights and Democracy, another agency that operates at arm's length from the government, faces internal division after new board members appointed by the Conservative government challenged its financial support for several organizations critical of the Israeli government's human rights record. A couple of board members have resigned in protest at what they see as ideological censorship.[43] Those who voice different sides of the development story are being silenced. The message to the NGO community is to follow government ideology or lose essential funding.

But there is a cost to this one-dimensional monologue. Nigerian novelist Chimamanda Adichie talks about the "danger of the single story": how relating only one aspect of a story flattens reality, robs people of dignity, and makes equality impossible.[44] She explains that the narrative created by a single story is not necessarily untrue but is incomplete. She also refers to Chinua Achebe, another Nigerian novelist, who calls for a "balance of stories" to round out the full experience of existence rather than levelling out life with a single narrative.[45] By analyzing the development experience, both within its historical and sociopolitical context and through the lived experiences of people, our narrative becomes fuller and more complete. The narrative of Canadian aid, with its annual budget of $4 billion, is likewise placed in context.

These trends in Canada's foreign affairs are an underlying and unflattering aspect of the story of aid. Politics form the backdrop to the work of all Canadian international development organizations and practitioners, regardless of how directly they depend on federal funding. In analyzing their experience in international development, contributors to this book start to recognize the context in which they operate. Such recognition moulds an analysis of the social space they inhabit while working in this sector. Through their stories, they interrogate their social location by examining their position in the world relative to that of others. This includes reflecting on class, race, gender, language, religion, power, privilege, stereotypes, and many other social factors that determine how people interact. Through this process, it becomes clear that the writers of *Generation NGO* are deeply attracted to human-centred development approaches, approaches that value empowering the poor, concentrating resources at the lower end of the social structure, promoting environmental sustainability, and embracing women and oppressed peoples as vital development players.

Reflecting on their experiences and the larger context of development aid, the contributors move beyond a single narrative of "the other" to delve deeper into the multiple stories of people's lives. This is the beginning of a differentiation between charity and solidarity, between a moral imperative to "help" those less fortunate and a more radical and effective call to stand shoulder to shoulder against injustice, collectively forging an agenda for action. Through their stories, our writers discover that solidarity is never simple, that there is an inherent tension in positions of power and privilege: "You can't dispose of privilege—that's a dangerous fantasy. It just can't be done. Privilege can only be creatively deployed."[46] While eschewing easy answers, these stories offer a starting point for others who share these questions and experiences. They share the journey of becoming more informed about what passes for development and offer some reflections on how to deploy privilege creatively as they strive to balance the one-sided narrative that reflects too uncritically on the story of Canada's hand in international development. From middle-class suburbs in Canada to refugee camps in Thailand and Ghana, these stories share the joy and pain that come with a loss of innocence and an awakened understanding of our global world.

1

Walls Topped with Broken Glass

On Privilege

Pike Krpan

From the first day I began my university education in international development studies, I learned that the rich are getting richer and the poor poorer. Rich, richer. Poor, poorer. The phrase became the mantra of my studies. It became a cliché. I read the stats on poverty over and over again, but they didn't seem real. Surrounded by the stone walls of my Canadian university, the facts seemed unrelated to the world of privilege I knew first hand. So as part of my studies I travelled to Ecuador in 2000 for a year of research.

I first became politicized about inequality when I participated in a youth exchange to Cuba. It so profoundly affected me that I decided to devote my postsecondary education to the subject. I spent a few years in university, crunching the numbers of poverty. I studied economics, political systems, modernization, and development theories that talked about the differences between two groups: the developed and underdeveloped, or the rich and poor. Studying was hard work, but it never revealed much to me about who I was. So when I arrived in Ecuador, that small South American nation ridged with the spine of the Andes, I never expected to learn the most about the group that was the most like me: Ecuador's middle class. Trudging a narrow path along the precipice to poverty and with a steep climb to wealth and security, this middle class had been invisible to me during my studies. Why had I been so unaware?

Studying "development" in university, I had always imagined myself to be on the side of the righteous: on the side of the poor. My studies were a catalyst for an outspoken and save-the-world type like me. Working in international development also promised an exotic escape from my humdrum, white suburban world. Once equipped with theory, I felt ready to travel far and right the wrongs I saw everywhere. I moved to a small suburban city, Sangolquí, just outside the Ecuadorean capital city of Quito. My Canadian university ran a small field school there, and the Canadian students were boarded with local families. I had envisioned dirt floors, big pots of food boiling on the stove, and washing our laundry by hand. This was not the case. My hosts, the Chamorro family, arrived to fetch me in their midsized car, with hair neatly combed, clothing decidedly Western, and their Spanish clean and polished. What had I really been expecting?

Vicente Chamorro worked as a government clerk and his wife, Gloria, as a teacher: stable and respectable but not especially well-paid professions. Their son, Carlos, twenty-five, lived with his wife and young child in an apartment on the top level of the house. Their daughter, Cecilia, twenty-one, attended university in nearby Quito. A young girl of fourteen, Veronica, a student whom Gloria had "adopted" from the school where she taught, lived in the back bedroom of the house. In exchange for room, board, and school tuition, she attended to household chores for the family.

On the night of my arrival, Gloria placed a ring of keys in my hand, beginning the painstaking task of showing me how to enter the house.

From the street, the Chamorro home was mostly obscured by high, whitewashed walls topped with Coke bottle shards, set upright in concrete. The house was a fortress. Before approaching the small entryway set in the high wall it was necessary to scan the street to be sure no dogs or strange men were lurking. Gloria called them *ladrones*—thieves. It wasn't easy to see the street. The warm light cast by the houses didn't reach it. I had already collided with the guy wire that supported the telephone pole outside the house, which was not encircled in yellow cautionary plastic like in Canada. (And so I found myself making the first of many comparisons, the phrase "not like in Canada" beginning its haunting of my thoughts.)

But our residential street was usually deserted. It was cold and unfriendly, lined on either side with walls, gates, and snarling guard dogs. At times, the dogs would run free, and I was instructed to carry a stone in my pocket to threaten them if approached.

The gate in the wall opened with a good shoulder push after tossing the tumblers of two different locks. Next, we approached the side door of the house, covered by a wrought-iron gate with a padlock. After opening this gate, we wrestled with two more locks on the actual door. All the windows of the house had wrought-iron lattice. Even the small room I slept in off the kitchen had its own lock. When Gloria and I finally entered the house, we were greeted by a jittery Vicente, who had crept silently downstairs to be sure we were not thieves trying to steal inside. His evening chore was to check and re-check all the locks in the house.

It was a privilege to be given the keys to the Chamorro house— only a specific few could enter.

This ritual of entering the house began to signify a border crossing from the public world to the private world I shared with my host family. It was a border that each family member was committed to policing, as they could not afford to hire a security guard. It was the differences on the two sides of that border that threw Ecuador's social and cultural context most boldly into relief. I thought I had challenged many of my own borders in preparing for my journey south: by broadening my educational landscape, by choosing to relinquish comfort for a world of unknowns, and by leaving expectations behind. But that aspect of my life most invisible to me, my middle-class background, silently accompanied me.

Of course, I didn't see it there at first.

Growing up in Canada, I was always fiercely ambitious and I had a solid sense of my own possibility. Middle-class people, my parents owned our detached house in a small Prairie city. If I wanted something, like piano lessons, a swim club membership, or a year abroad as a high school exchange student, my parents could afford it. I was a daydreamer as a child, with visions of great adventures for myself, never of domesticity. I was encouraged to travel alone at a young age. My independence had always been instrumental to my development as a person. It carried me to Ecuador. Wrapped in this image of myself, I went out through the locked doors of the Chamorro house to explore my new world.

The street was unappealing to the Chamorros. From the beginning, they were confused by my constant wish to go out. While they exhorted me to steer clear of certain areas and worried for my well-being, for me the foreignness of the street was a pull to adventure. I could see why they were worried, since a white woman walking alone attracted attention, both innocent and opportunistic. Most often, I found the experience exhilarating. I walked the streets with extra senses. New pores opened to the stench of marketplaces. Alert hairs stood on end when barking dogs approached me. Black crud from diesel buses lodged in my nostrils. I sensed a new, expanded periphery of my vision and felt the shadows in every darkened doorstep.

Even with the exhilaration, I also felt isolated. I was concerned to see so few women walking in the streets of Sangolquí, especially as night fell. Except in the market area, there were rarely any people about. There were no street signs and few landmarks. Groups of men would gather in small squares, passing bottles back and forth. The quick equatorial descent of the sun would heighten the sense of urgency to hurry home. Passing women were often subjected to catcalls, whistles, and gawking. I would ask for directions to my street,

Calle Chimborazo. No one had heard of it even though many times, I was only a few lanes away. How could it be that they did not know the streets in their own community? I wondered.

I posed this and many other questions to the Chamorros. They did not have any ready answers. The people on Ecuador's streets were as foreign to them as they were to me, and they were suspicious of everyone they did not know. They cautioned me that people on the street were risky, prone to ugliness, even violence. Even so, for me these unknowns held a clue about the social division between poor and rich, a division I perceived as a simple barrier of ignorance. If I could study development and relate to the poor, why couldn't the Chamorros?

The Chamorros saw people in the street as poor, dirty, and *indio*. This was in direct contrast to my impression that all Ecuadoreans were of mixed European and indigenous heritage: *mestizos*. At first, their common dark hair and smoky eyes, short stature, and brownish skin allowed me to classify them, abstractly, as a "people." Slowly, however, the collection of details that made up a person's racial and class status in that country became visible to me. The most potent sign was the poncho. Not just a manner of dress to stay warm in the thin mountain air, the poncho was a bold Indian symbol, along with the colourful beaded strands that the indigenous women wound around their wrists and necks. Few Ecuadoreans dressed this way in suburban Sangolquí. My host mother, Gloria, regularly pointed out to me that her skin was very white and delicate. She asked me to send high-protection sunscreen from Canada on my return. She compared her nose to mine, proudly noting their common European ridges. By contrast, Veronica, the fourteen-year-old girl they boarded, had darker skin. Although she was introduced to me as a surrogate daughter, the Chamorros did not treat Veronica like their other children. She had a plain, simple room, with no special furnishings. When a close family member married, everyone got new clothes except Veronica. I held her as she cried over feeling old-fashioned and ugly.

In Sangolquí, I took a course in Quechua, Ecuador's most widely spoken indigenous language. One of the first words I learned was *runa*, the Quechua word for people, as in "our people." But in local conquistador Spanish, the word meant something cheap, of poor quality. As I ate dinner with the Chamorros, I explained the Quechua meaning of *runa*. "You mean that Veronica is *runa*?" Carlos joked. They all laughed, except Veronica. Her face reddened as she stood by the kitchen sink, standing up, eating her dinner. Later that night she told me that as a child she would stay up all night and knit wool sweaters to sell to tourists with her mother. She had not seen her mother in many years.

These incidents gave me clues about the divide between the poor, indigenous class and the middle class, which sought to distance itself from any symbols of mixed heritage. My middle-class family's approach was to remain at home, where they were comfortable and insulated.

I rarely saw Cecilia, Gloria and Vicente's daughter, on the bus into the city, although we both frequently travelled there. Many buses went to Quito, each with different prices and people boarding them. I would jump on the first bus to barrel through town. Cecilia always took the special bus that travelled a direct route to the city's prosperous university area. As a young woman, she would almost never walk in the streets alone. To ensure her safety, her brother would drive her to a special bus stop and pick her up there on her return, even though it was just a ten-minute walk away.

But I could not stay in or depend on rides from my host family. I wanted to go out and visit friends in the evening, or have a beer near the church plaza, or go dancing in the city. In part, this desire to experience it all was fuelled by my feminist ideals. I noticed, early on, that my social group was composed of Canadian men and women and Ecuadorean men, but not Ecuadorean women. My community activism in Canada had been devoted to women's safety and representation in public spaces. Now it seems a bit foolish, but at the time I felt I was directly confronting male dominance on behalf of Ecuadorean women. I wanted to stir things up.

I started by interviewing Cecilia. She was confused by my questions. "Why would I want to go out at night, especially by myself?" she asked. She preferred to stay at home with family or friends. "Where would I go?" There were no dance clubs or movie theatres in Sangolquí. If she did want to go somewhere, she could ask her father or brother to drive her there. But as I pressed her and others to talk about walking in the streets, fears rose up. They were not the ones I expected.

While Canadian women told me quite bluntly that they were afraid of being raped, all the Ecuadoreans told me they were afraid of being robbed. The Canadians told me how they attempted safety. They walked in the middle of the street to avoid men jumping out from dark corners. They wore "shoes to run in." They carried keys clenched between their fingers to stab attackers. To them, the catcalls were seduction attempts that could easily go wrong. Ecuadorean women make themselves safer by removing their watches, necklaces, rings, and other jewellery. I asked my Ecuadorean friend Gaby what she thought of my walking alone at night. While I worried that I would be perceived as a sexually promiscuous foreigner, Gaby was concerned for my safety because people would assume I was a *rich* foreigner. I asked Gaby if it bothered her to be whistled at. She brushed it off as juvenile. She explained that men needed to defend their manhood by pretending to seduce women on the street. This was a game that men played as they got drunk to avoid confronting each other.

Pressing on, I asked what could be done to make the streets of Sangolquí safer for women. Canadian women suggested improved street lighting and legislation to prevent drinking in certain public places. But Ecuadoreans had difficulty answering the question. Many explained that they already had strategies in place for their safety. Their brothers and fathers drove them home. Under my repeated questioning, one suggested hiring a private guard for every corner.

The Ecuadorean middle-class women saw the street as a dirty place for poor people who did not have the financial means to build safe homes. They preferred to stay home. I persisted. Wasn't oppression in the home the reason for women's liberation in the first place?

It was becoming clear that my questions weren't promoting feminism at all. My feminist ideas were a hard sell. Ecuadorean women were fearful of poverty, not of being forced to bake too many cookies. They were not uncomfortable with or upset by the code of gendered behaviour they were expected to follow—I was!

As a white feminist, I romanticized the street as a battleground of human rights, just as I imagined myself taking bold steps for womankind. I think we all create these mini-fictions as development workers as a way to keep faith, forge ahead, and believe our own good intentions. My street exploration was a form of defiance. My mythological ideal of an integrated community, with children playing happily in parks, was falsely coloured by my own suburban childhood. I had learned to ride a bike on a gentle cul-de-sac where cars rarely passed. As the streetlights came on, my mother would call me from the doorstep of our house, her voice tinged with annoyance (never fear) that I was not returning before dusk as she had asked. This middle-class reverie of open bay windows and lawns in orderly rows—the dream by which North America is so inexplicably and poisonously entranced—was not happening in Ecuador. Even though I was well aware of the suburban pretence of happiness and its false ring for the future, I still carried a naïve sense of its idealism with me. I had directly benefited from the enclave mentality of suburban North America, even as I became more aware of how my neighbourhood was not accessible to all: it was exclusively white and middle class; strangers were noted and chased off with a subtlety that escaped my childhood eyes.

But there was no subtlety in Ecuador. In Sangolquí, there were no green parks populated by swing sets and jungle gyms. There was only the concrete town square, run by poor shoeshine boys as young as five years old, their brightly coloured acrylic sweaters stained by grease. On my street, an empty lot was a garbage dump and served as forage for a few cows. The walls were the silent faces of a people afraid of each other. Hiding, this middle class had abandoned the street to the poor. The visible symbols of exclusion in Ecuador jumped out at me. But still I struggled to relate them to my own middle-class experience growing up.

For the Chamorros, the high walls temporarily erased the looming possibility of poverty. But it is only a few steps away. In his 1991

The Book of Embraces, Eduardo Galeano says the walls speak. In a time of crisis, graffiti forms the conversations that people no longer have with each other. He quotes a message painted at the entrance to one of the poorest neighbourhoods of Caracas, Venezuela: "Welcome, middle class." This fear of abject poverty manifests itself in everyday conversation, newspaper accounts, and television. Politicians rail against it, while perpetuating it, as do police and petty bureaucrats. At the dinner table, the Chamorros would try to trump each other's stories of theft in the neighbourhood. Theft is nothing new. In Ecuador, theft is history. Little known on the world stage because of its lack of headline-grabbing dictatorships and revolutions, Ecuador has undergone a less dramatic and grinding form of colonialism. The theft of resources by banana exporters, oil giants, and tourists has been almost imperceptible to the rest of the world. The poor indigenous routinely lose it all and then start anew, creating something out of nothing.

But in the many years of resource exploitation, a small group grasped the dirty tail end of prosperity. Ecuador's middle class built a precarious small something, and those glittering glass shards along my garden wall protected it. A lack of faith in public institutions like the police and the government means that every family fends for itself, building a fortress of its own from those who would take it.

One morning, I saw the middle-class fortress approach writ large on a new billboard towering above bent workers trundling wheelbarrows of dirt and concrete. It was dominated by the image of a large keyhole, with a nightmarish landlord intrusively peeking through it toward the viewer. Accompanying text promised a goodbye to landlords and hello to your own home, from US$13,000. In the landlord's sneer, the Chamorros' fears were made real. The billboard promised a retreat to safety, to a neighbourhood with extra locks, guard dogs, and private security guards to patrol the street. Exploiting a sense of fear, the keyhole showed the division between poor and violent public spaces and parcelled-out private homes. Appealing to a desire for privacy and independence, the real message of this sign was: be afraid.

The keyhole was the narrow passageway between the haves and have-nots. It was through this keyhole I tried to pass whenever I was coming and going from the Chamorro household. Thinking I was just a helpful and knowledgeable outsider, I assumed I could easily slip through. But fumbling with all those locks so many times, I started to understand my discomfort with crossing the security border into my house. It was impossible to unlock all those doors neutrally and pass as an unconditional supporter of the poor. I was slowly becoming aware of this middle class as my own.

In Canada, my social class had been invisible to me. My middle-class experiences and reality were commonly represented on television, in newspapers, and on CBC radio. I could easily think that everyone lived that way. Like the Chamorros, I had dismissed poor people as thieves—or, to use North American lingo, "welfare bums" who were stealing money from hard-working people. I swallowed racist stereotypes about the indigenous people who were sequestered on reserves outside my home town. Resource exploration in Canada—farming, mining, oil development—were all processes that contributed, slowly but surely, to the dispossession of indigenous people and created the conditions to build the country's middle class. I had been led to believe that Native people had generously given white settlers this land, not been forced off it. These lies were my own middle-class heritage, not so different from those of Ecuador. The walls, locks, and broken glass all had their counterparts in Canada, but these had been invisible to me. My childhood neighbourhood was bordered by a thick hedge of history. It was also a fortress. The locks, guards, and dogs were built into Canada's laws, educational system, government, and official language policies. I saw this fortress only when I returned from Ecuador.

Back in Canada, the beautiful public parks I so fondly remembered were silently policed by security cameras. The cameras did not catch criminals but instead deterred those who did not "belong." Homeless people were chased from resting places in public parks by police, expected to move along with all their belongings and continually re-create a new home. In the streets, I saw police harassing street kids to stop panhandling in the tourist area. I remembered those shoeshine boys in Ecuador. At least they had been left alone to make a small living. Who was I kidding? Street kids in Canada had as little faith in the police or the legal system as Ecuadoreans did. The world over, such institutions didn't serve the interests of the poor. Even their name— *street kids*—showed how Canada, too, had abandoned people to so-called public space, the home of homelessness.

In Canada, I became a member of an anti-poverty group. I realized I had had no friends who were not middle-class when I was growing up. We worked on campaigns to address the ridiculously low levels of social and disability assistance available to the unemployed and unemployable. If injured or beset by illness, Canada's middle class is also only a few steps from poverty. They rarely see this until it is too late. Our social successes of universal health care and education are held up as triumphs when we compare ourselves to other countries, even as they are under increasing attack by privatization. That trumpeting precludes deeper insight into the continuing problems of poverty, exclusion, and racism that run so deep in Canada, particularly for Native people.

It took travelling to Ecuador for me even to *see* poverty at home. Seduced by a dream of adventure, I studied the poverty of those far away. In Ecuador, I was disappointed that the Chamorros did not understand a word of Quechua and did not have any sympathy for or understanding of indigenous people. But I knew not a word of Cree, the language of the people on whose land I grew up, or of any other indigenous Canadian language.

I had been travelling through borders every day in Canada, but because of the privilege I enjoyed as a middle-class white woman, they had been completely invisible. At birth, I had already been given a big ring of keys. I had travelled through doors of privilege easily because of my social class and race. My development education did not encourage me to consider my own historical position as a white European settler, or the ongoing genocidal effects of that settlement, which has created grinding poverty for the indigenous people of Turtle Island. Neither did it encourage me to see Native peoples in Canada as survivors and resisters, even though I could romanticize every road block made in political protest in Ecuador.

I think it was Nelson Mandela who said there is nothing like returning to a place that remains unchanged to find the ways in which you have changed. My experiences in international development made me realize that the social problems I could readily identify and desire to change in other countries are happening in Canada as well. My education had been primarily a training ground for professionalized international charity. I finished my education, calling it "CIDA prep school." Middle-class students like me were taught that only they had the knowledge and skills to intervene and "fix" the problems of international poverty. Plus, they got a degree that ensured they would get paid well to attempt it. Often enough, that perspective creates and perpetuates inequality. Only rarely did my education cultivate the consciousness needed for solidarity, and that was when I practised justice in my own backyard. My "saving the world" complex was saturated with a desire for the exotic. Recognizing poverty in my own country made me uncomfortable, as it forced me to think about how I and my family and friends deny the truth of our society and its problems. In Canada, too, the rich are getting richer and the poor poorer. But siding with the poor is not as easy when you realize that you directly benefit from theft from the poor. Things are more complicated when you see how you are implicated in the impoverishment of others who are close to home.

I still struggle with this knowledge, and with the question of how to wield the power of my privilege. I think that I will struggle with it until inequality no longer exists. In the meantime, I'm working every day to see my own walls topped with broken glass. I guess you could say I'm working on my own development.

2

Adding Things up in Namibia

Zoe Kahn

Namibia is not a particularly evocative word for most Canadians. Some know it as the name of an African country; others have never heard of it. For me though, the word Namibia instantly transports me to a place and a formative experience I remain intensely grateful for. Namibia broke my heart, but I love it for all the fundamental lessons it taught me about the world and my place in it.

I had always wanted to go to Africa, although I find it hard to explain why. Perhaps because it seemed to be a completely different world. My knowledge of the continent was rather haphazard and by no means extensive. I had seen a hundred horrifying images of the 1980s Ethiopian famine and knew by heart all the words to Live Aid's "Do They Know It's Christmas?" I had listened to the stories of a great-aunt who had spent ten years working in Malawi and Zambia. As a high school student, I had taken part in a World Vision hunger strike known as the 30 Hour Famine. I must have known about the genocide in Rwanda, although probably not in any great detail. For me, Africa was a place where bad things happened to people who seemed unable to help themselves, whom we could and should try to help. It amazes me now just how little I knew or understood.

I arrived in Namibia in October 1997, a few months after completing my teaching degree. For reasons that became less clear as my degree progressed, I had majored in mathematics, and from there teaching had seemed like an obvious choice. However, as I neared the end of my degree, the idea of applying to local school boards terrified me and the wider world beckoned. While I had been very excited to attend an international teaching fair, it failed to offer what I was looking for. There were lots of jobs available, even some in Africa, but they entailed either joining other international staff in teaching elite and expatriate youth or becoming one of a handful of much-heralded and overpaid foreign teachers among an understandably resentful national staff. Neither option appealed to me so I continued to look for different ones.

I knew absolutely nothing about the world of international development, but I immediately identified with the vision and mission statement of an organization called Voluntary Service Overseas (VSO). Among other things, VSO serves as a kind of recruitment agency for developing countries and works to find qualified volunteers to fill job placements that cannot be filled locally. When VSO offered me a position teaching at the government-run Maria Mwengere Secondary School in northern rural Namibia, I immediately accepted.

Prior to receiving the job posting, I was unaware of Namibia's existence. When I looked at an atlas, I was initially slightly disappointed that Namibia was quite a distance from the equator as I thought it meant cooler weather. I accepted the placement having no concept of the country's history or geography, and no real idea of what my living conditions would be. Would I have electricity? Would I be living in a house? Would I be the only expatriate teacher there? When people asked me these kinds of questions, more often than not I did not have answers.

I arrived in Namibia as a twenty-three-year-old recent university graduate with relatively little life experience and absolutely no experience living overseas. In retrospect, I am embarrassed at the combination of idealistic naïveté and arrogance that took me there. But I have come to view my general lack of life experience and global awareness as a positive thing as it set the stage for the learning that followed. I had thought the world to be a pretty fair place but almost immediately I struggled to reconcile this belief with new experiences that more than hinted that the world had glaring inconsistencies. I found myself on a learning curve that was steep and at times hard to navigate.

AFRICA FOR BEGINNERS

Namibia is a large country situated to the north and west of South Africa. It became a German protectorate in 1884, but after the First World War the League of Nations (the precursor to the United Nations) mandated South African rule for the relatively under-populated country. Although the United Nations abolished this mandate in 1966, South Africa rebelled and years of military struggle between the two countries culminated in Namibian independence in 1990. Until that time, Namibia was essentially treated as a South African province, in which the predominantly non-white inhabitants were subject to the same apartheid laws as their neighbours to the south.

When Namibia gained independence, it was a bit of a shock for all involved. A number of events had persuaded beleaguered South African president P.W. Botha to relinquish Namibia rather suddenly, and the existing systems and infrastructure did not allow for an entirely smooth transition to democracy. Prompt decisions were necessarily made about some fundamental issues, and the choices made with respect to language and education strongly influenced my teaching experience. For example, as Afrikaans was deemed to be the language of the oppressor (white South Africa), English was declared Namibia's official language although only a small percentage of the population understood or spoke it. Moreover, in an effort to replace the discriminatory apartheid education system quickly, Namibia adopted the British-based International General Certificate of Secondary Education (IGCSE).

Under the apartheid education system, math and science had been deemed subjects that non-whites had little need for and consequently, many teachers graduated from this system with poor skills in those subjects and little desire or ability to teach them. This led to non-Namibians, frequently from the Northern hemisphere, being engaged to teach at the more senior levels. Upon my arrival in Namibia, I joined the fairly substantial group of expatriate teachers on whom the Namibian Ministry of Basic Education relied to make up for the shortfall in local English, math, and science teachers.

Thinking back to my first days in Namibia's capital city, it is easy to see why the country is often called "Africa for Beginners." Windhoek did not look very different from any other small city I had visited. The streets were wide and paved, and although I was in the midst of a desert there were lots of manicured green areas and flower gardens. There were shopping malls, movie theatres, mini-golf, even Kentucky Fried Chicken. Not surprisingly, my two weeks of "orientation" flew by and before I knew it I was sitting nervously in a car heading some eight hundred kilometres north, to a place I would soon call home.

CROSSING THE LINE

The main road leading to northern Namibia is paved and abnormally straight; it was put in by the South Africans to serve as a runway for army planes. The drive is made interesting only by the terrain changes; as the climate changes from desert to semi-tropical, the almost lunar landscape becomes much more colourful and varied. My first drive was also made interesting by the driver who had been sent to collect me. His Ministry of Education vehicle beeped whenever the car exceeded a hundred kilometres an hour, which he countered by turning the radio volume up to the highest level possible.

In fewer hours than was legal, we arrived at what is known as the Red Line, often said to separate the First World from the Third in Namibia. While the north–south length of the country is close to fifteen hundred kilometres, the majority of the inhabitants reside in the approximately two-hundred-kilometre strip of land that lies between Red Line and the northern border. During colonialism and then apartheid, the Line served as a social, economic, and physical barrier that separated the tribal lands up north from the predominantly white-owned and -controlled cattle and game ranches in the southern region. Today, Namibians living above the Red Line no longer require special permission to cross, but it still serves as a veterinary checkpoint and can prevent northern farmers from getting access to the main agricultural markets and prime farming land. This is justified by the increased prevalence of diseases in the more tropical north, something I first learned about during my pre-travel health briefing.

After crossing this famous Red Line, I saw more of the Africa I expected. Homesteads made of mud and straw appeared on both sides of the highway, their owners often either sitting on plastic chairs outside them or tending plots nearby. Every now and then we passed stalls selling anything from vegetables to local handiwork. We also passed a number of primary schools and what I soon came to know as *kuka* shops, tin shacks that sold primarily cool drinks, beer, and washing powder. My favourite building was a mud hut that had "Emmy was born to suffer" painted in large black letters on the wall.

MY HOME AWAY FROM HOME

Eight hours after leaving Windhoek, we arrived at Maria Mwengere Secondary School, commonly known as Maria. Built soon after independence and located about fifteen kilometres outside the small town of Rundu, it housed most of the twenty-five teachers and six hundred students within its fenced grounds. Maria's newness made it a poster child for the Kavango region, where actual educational achievements lagged behind other Namibian regions. Consequently, Maria's staff came from all over the country and also from South Africa, Zimbabwe, Zambia, and Nigeria. When I arrived, I replaced a British VSO who had spent three years there as the head of mathematics and had loved almost every minute of it. I, too, would come to love living at Maria, although the feeling was initially somewhat hard won. I spent my first few weeks living in town and had mixed feelings about moving out to the rural school campus when housing became available.

Maria is situated right on the border with Angola. It is part of a small village called Kayengona that sits on the banks of the Kavango River. The river separates the two countries and is narrow enough for people to have conversations across it as they collect water or wash their clothes and bodies. A borehole serves the water needs of Maria and the health clinic next door, but while I lived there residents of the local village had sporadic access at best to the on-site pump. This meant that they relied on the river, which was not particularly clean and was also home to crocodiles and hippos. Most people, including myself, knew of at least one person who had had a nasty experience with one of these inhabitants.

With the departure of the previous VSO volunteer, I became the only white person in Kayengona. Understandably, I was a bit of a novelty. At a time when I would have loved to fly under the radar, there was no way to do so. My world was for the most part restricted to this small community. When the need to have some "me" time was overwhelming, I took late afternoon walks down by the river. I know I made a strange sight: a young, Walkman-wearing white woman striding purposefully about in what was clearly not her usual milieu. Occasionally, a truck full of backpackers would pass me on the way to set up camp at a lodge some twenty kilometres up the road. I enjoyed the confused looks on their faces as they happened upon me.

A WHOLE NEW WORLD?

Although it looked nothing like the high schools back in Canada, Maria was quite a well-resourced school. It was made up of four rows of one-storey blocks that housed the administration offices, science labs, classrooms, and other staff facilities. These blocks were separated by gardens, and each class was responsible for tending the plot in front of it. I had a fairly standard classroom with concrete floors and walls, windows, a teacher's wooden desk, and about forty student desks and chairs. Although the rooms were equipped with overhead lights and power outlets, controlling the temperature entailed purchasing either a fan (in the summer) or a block heater (in the winter). My classroom also had a locked storage room in which to keep books and supplies. Maria had a photocopier that was put to good use, and the principal had a computer in his office. Sometimes it was used for word processing, but mostly it facilitated his solitaire habit. The school did have a phone, but it was on a party line and not very reliable, so many teachers chose to purchase cell phones and drive toward town to get a signal to pick up messages. I had to rely on the farm line, which proved very frustrating at times, but the immense feeling of satisfaction I got upon successfully making a call almost made the hassle worthwhile. Never before or since has the act of making a telephone call elicited such a range of emotions or in itself constituted having a good day.

Once I got used to my new normality and into the daily routine of teaching, it was easy to forget that I was living in a different world. Little things reminded me though, like the time I collected garbage with my students. There was a lot of litter floating around Maria's grounds, in part because people were unused to things that could not be returned to the environment. When the school administration decided that classes should spend an hour or so cleaning up the grounds, I was responsible for holding the garbage bag for my class. I was confused at how heavy it soon became but discovered that the weight of the bag was directly related to the number of rocks in it. Looking to one of my students I asked, "Why are rocks in here? We want to fill it with garbage: stuff that doesn't belong out here."

He replied, "But Miss, when we are not wearing shoes these rocks are always hurting our feet. They are garbage." I could see his point so continued to lug the bag around.

COMFORT LEVELS

I taught six classes in my first year: four grade 10 classes and one each of grades 11 and 12. My grade 10 classes each had about forty students, a fairly equal mix of males and females. We spent the year preparing for a national exam that would evaluate their last three years of cumulative learning. My grade 11 class, made up of the thirty students (six of them female) who had passed the math exam the year before, undertook the first year of the two-year IGSCE program. My predominantly male grade 12 class prepared for the final IGSCE exam. I soon learned that marked gender discrepancies were a hallmark of the Kavango region, where male students tended to outperform their female counterparts in all the sciences. It seemed generally accepted that girls were not particularly good at these subjects and that this mattered little as they had scarce need for them. I tried to address this through my teaching style and by arranging for gender-specific math lessons.

For my grade 10 classes, deciding what to teach was a challenge. A set curriculum was in place, but many learners did not have the basic math skills needed to master it. A lot of them had long since stopped trying to learn math and viewed the subject as a huge jumble of unrelated facts. I attribute this mostly to the sad truth that many students had never had the benefit of a qualified math teacher. Still, focusing on the basics meant neglecting the curriculum they were to be evaluated on and the needs of those students who were ready to learn it. While trying to meet the varied needs of students is a juggling act for any teacher, it certainly felt as though I was facing this on an unprecedented scale. I felt overwhelmed, depressed, and extremely frustrated when students failed to make the progress I knew they were capable of.

But the juggling act was not the only challenge I faced. I was also up against the task of teaching a curriculum that was largely irrelevant to the lives of my students. When I started at Maria, I was relieved to find that the curriculum was similar to the Canadian one. But after talking with a Zimbabwean colleague one day, I began to question the wisdom of this. After all, was it not strange that a teacher from

Africa could rhyme off the main exports of British Columbia when I could not? He explained to me that he had learned about Canadian exports while in school, when rather than learning about the history and geography of Zimbabwe, he had memorized all manner of facts about the larger British empire. I immediately compared this with how little I had learned about Africa during my formal education.

In fact, while most North Americans I knew were unable to say much about Namibia, my Namibian students could tell me a lot about America. Thanks to the curriculum, American music, movies, and entertainment magazines, all too often Namibians seemed to view North America the way eight-year-olds view Disneyland. I tried to give a more realistic depiction of my home continent to help them realize that it was far from the utopia they pictured. It was an uphill battle though, as many students refused to conceive of white people being poor and were reluctant to believe that Michael Jordan or Tupac Shakur were not representative of an average African American experience. I somewhat romantically believed that "living in poverty" in Africa was a better reality than "living in poverty" in America, but I came to appreciate the factors that made my students think otherwise.

All of this helped me to understand that when it came to culture, I should probably feel uncomfortable with the comfortable and with anything that seemed to reflect my experiences more closely than those of the Namibians around me. My students had a history and culture of their own, and the skills and knowledge they needed to succeed in the lives they would lead were undoubtedly different from what was required by students in Canada, for example. So why was so much of the curriculum so irrelevant to their daily lives? Why was it so theoretical and unconnected to their realities? During one oral English exam, students were asked to speak about space travel. It seemed unreasonable to expect this of students living in an agricultural society.

While I was unable to get my head around all the different issues at play, I began to feel less and less comfortable with teaching a Northern-centric curriculum in Africa. Was I not just reinforcing an unjust world order that cast the Northern hemisphere as a role model that the rest of the world should strive for? I worried that threaded throughout my teaching were all kinds of subliminal messages about what development was and what should be done with the lessons I was giving. I started to feel like an unwitting missionary of Northern beliefs and values, and was unsure of how this was truly serving my learners or helping Namibia "develop" on its own terms.

THE WEAKER SEX . . .

Ideological issues aside, my biggest challenge with the senior grades was to convince male students that they should listen to an opinionated white woman who was not much older than themselves. It caused me no end of frustration and self-doubt when less dedicated male colleagues effortlessly got male students to comply with homework requests while I faced a constant struggle. Things got a little better in the second year, when the grade 12 class learned that the six female learners had all placed in the top group of students. This was not because they were more capable than their male counterparts, or because of any favouritism on my part; it was entirely because they had been more willing to complete the tasks I had assigned the year before.

When it came to pushing for gender equality, Maria's teachers were in no way leading the charge. Gender roles among our mostly male staff were both defined and engrained. Our monthly staff birthday celebrations were a great example. As the teachers sat around the perimeter of the staff lounge and waited to be served, the women were skipped over until every man in the room had a plate in front of him. Of greater concern, questionable relationships between male staff and female students were silently tolerated while technically forbidden. The Zambian agriculture teacher once took the time to explain to me that while one was looking after the cow, it was only fair to get some "free milk."

In speaking out on gender issues, I was exercising a level of freedom as a foreigner that my female colleagues could only dream of. Much to their active encouragement and enjoyment, I pushed and questioned things they could not. I was an outsider and by pretending not to understand things, I like to think I encouraged colleagues to rethink the status quo. I felt both pride and despair when the more timid of my two housemates forcefully told a male colleague that once she married, she would not get up to heat her husband's dinner if he came home very late. She would, however, make sure his clothes were ready for the next morning as "she knew her duty." I have to admit to feeling much more kinship with my other housemate. She was a force to be reckoned with, and though many of the male teachers talked a good game about a number of things, they didn't do it quite so loudly when she was around.

Namibian men were both fascinated and confused by my ideas about gender equality. This was made especially clear during an overnight stay at a traditional homestead in the neighbouring Ovambo region. It had taken over an hour of off-road driving to reach the *kraal*, a collection of buildings and huts surrounded by a wooden fence. We spent the evening sitting around an open fire at the local *kuka* shop with some local men and got into a heated debate on gender roles. The general opinion was that while women were just as smart as men, their physical weakness made them inferior. This made me laugh as I often saw women walking down a dusty road with children on their backs and loads balanced on their heads while their husbands walked beside unburdened. At the end of the evening, one of the men turned to me and said in a somewhat resigned fashion, "I think you would be a friend to Oprah." I would like to believe that this meant I made some sort of positive impression on them, but I am still not convinced it was intended as a compliment.

THERE'S MORE TO LIFE THAN SCHOOL

While at Maria I was fairly isolated from the outside world: shopping or swimming or socializing with other VSOs meant a trip into Rundu. To get there, I either had to secure a ride with a fellow teacher or walk down to the main dirt road to hitchhike. More often than not, I hitched.

It was common practice that if drivers had space, they stopped to pick up paying passengers. The most common vehicle used was a pickup truck, or *bakkie*, as it was generally known.

I spent many a trip to and from town sitting or standing in the back bed of an aging truck, squeezed in between fellow commuters, their babies, their possessions and occasionally, their livestock. On occasion, the whiteness of my skin would secure me a special seat in the front of the car. This proved a bit of an ethical dilemma: while it was a safer and more comfortable ride and promised a chance for some interesting conversation, I knew I was awarded it for inappropriate reasons. Sometimes I accepted gladly; at other times I had little choice. Perhaps the fact that I was sharing this common form of transport instantly conveyed that I was not one of "those" whites, the whites who had prospered under apartheid and had been reluctant to see it end. A man once told me that before independence, he sat in the back of the *bakkie* while his boss's dog enjoyed the front seat, regardless of the weather. While the memories were still fresh, there was nevertheless a remarkable climate of forgiveness given that independence had taken place barely ten years before.

White Namibians tended to embrace me as one of their own and were unfailingly welcoming, even if they could not quite grasp my reasons for being in Namibia. As long as I was standing by myself, or with another white person, they, too, would pick me up and offer a comfortable ride, generally in a shiny, air-conditioned car. Along with the comfort came an ethical dilemma: white drivers would very rarely stop to pick up black Namibians. When I first arrived, I was sure I would never accept a ride that was offered to me and not to a black counterpart. I never did in theory, but I learned that by hitching from less popular starting points I could have the best of both worlds. I could secure a safe ride while remaining in blissful ignorance of the driver's potential racism. White Namibians also had their stories of how things used to be prior to independence, and I am not sure they realized how absurd some of them sounded. One man explained wistfully that he had "always had hot water before independence." To me, the occasional cold shower seemed a relatively small price to pay to secure the rights of his compatriots.

Really though, white Namibians were as much a product of their upbringing as black Namibians, or as middle-class Canadians for that matter. During my first year at Maria, an Afrikaner woman (white South African) was one of the three deputy head teachers. Used to teaching in town, she had taken the position because of the promotion that went with it. It was clear from the beginning that she was not in her element, but she worked hard and took her duties seriously. After a couple of months, however, she decided to take a position in town that would cut down on her commute and allow her to be closer to her young children. She cried twice on her last day, both in a staff meeting when the principal paid tribute to her and then again at the school assembly after the students had sung her favourite song in effortless harmony. She was so moved that she had to make her way back to her office, and I followed her to see if she was all right. She turned to me with tears in her eyes and explained, "I just didn't think I could get so attached to black people." Welcome to post-apartheid Namibia.

THE MEANING OF LIFE

Over the years, various people have offered me their opinion that people in the developing world simply do not value life the way that we do in the North. I can only assume that they do not recognize the interconnectedness of the world or the very tangible ways in which lifestyles in the North come at the expense of lifestyles in the South. We live as we do because people in developing countries live as they do. So who is it that devalues the human experience? Northern countries continue to be reluctant to change trade structures that widen the gap between the world's rich and poor. Some are just as reluctant to halt the growing gap opening up between the rich and poor in their own countries. As Canadians we persist in seeing ourselves as charitable but have yet to muster the political will to honour a commitment we made in the 1970s to allocate just 0.7 per cent of our gross national income to international development aid. More than that, we do not always take the time to learn what the issues are. We are far more likely to write a cheque or give a cash donation in times of crisis than to understand and advocate for more fundamental and long-term solutions, such as fairer trade policies or debt forgiveness.

Death was a part of my life in Namibia in a way it had never been back in Canada. It was a rare week when I did not hear about the death of someone, and the most common causes were car accidents, malaria, and AIDS. In fact, student absenteeism (due predominantly to funeral attendance) proved so disruptive that at one school staff meeting we discussed implementing a policy to require students to produce a death certificate if they wanted to attend a funeral (theoretically ensuring that it was a significantly close family connection). It was all a little surreal for me and so different from Canada. I can still remember the death of a classmate's father when I was in grade 5, a hugely significant event for the whole school. But it could not be one in Namibia, if only because the sheer number of deaths made such a response infeasible.

During my time in Kavango, the HIV/AIDS infection rate was thought to be upward of 25 per cent (based on testing done at prenatal clinics). However, at that point people had yet to die in large numbers and so AIDS did not have the immediacy of other causes of death. When deaths from malaria or car accidents came so suddenly, it was all too easy to ignore something that might or might not kill you a few years down the road. Some Namibians seemed able to shrug off warnings about contracting HIV in the same way smokers shrug off warnings about lung cancer. All my students knew the facts about HIV/AIDS, but often this knowledge failed to translate itself into action. It was still a big deal for someone to admit publicly to being HIV positive, perhaps because it was seen primarily as a sexually transmitted disease and therefore not appropriate to discuss in public.

As aware as I thought I was, I was still taken completely by surprise when a recently married and pregnant female colleague died of AIDS. She had lost some weight in the preceding months and had taken an increasing number of sick days, but she attributed it to a pre-existing condition and I never questioned this. When my housemate confided at the start of a new term that she thought this teacher would not make it, I thought she was being dramatic. In my experience, young people did not just get sick and die. But sure enough, we received the news just two days later that she had died. While my housemate and I discussed the cause of her death, it seemed inappropriate to share with others what she had chosen to keep to herself. Perhaps we allowed a dangerous cycle to continue.

TROUBLED TIMES

Toward the end of my second year at Maria, life changed for most people in Rundu. The Namibian government gave Angolan forces access to the Namibian side of the river so that they could surround the rebel UNITA troops. All of a sudden there were patrols along the river and soldiers everywhere. A curfew was imposed, and it became normal for soldiers with guns to enforce it at local establishments. It was possible to witness gun fights taking place on the flood plains and there were frequent tales of nightly roundups in the villages along the river. When people failed to show their identity papers, they were arrested and held in what soon became a crowded local jail. This happened despite the fact that the border had been fluid for years and there was no real way of knowing who belonged where. Namibia's borders, after all, had been negotiated by colonial powers and not by the Africans who lived along them.

As the weeks passed, the situation in Kavango became increasingly unstable. When UNITA soldiers made their way over to the Namibian side in search of food and other supplies, they took to planting landmines. Namibians living in bordering villages and communities were killed or maimed going about the normal course of their lives. Eventually it was deemed unsafe for volunteers to remain in the area, but leaving was difficult. For all the upheaval and uncertainty going on around me, the changes to my life had actually been pretty minimal. I never felt I was in danger, although I was also aware that I had no real idea what this kind of danger should feel like. How could I? I had no frame of reference, which possibly made it foolish to trust any kind of gut feeling I had. This was an entirely new situation for me, but many Namibians had experienced similar insecurity before and were more resigned to it.

As the evacuation of volunteers became inevitable, I struggled to understand the many injustices. Why did I have the power to leave when so many of my friends and colleagues did not? Why would every effort be made to ensure the safety of international development workers while local people were left to the hands of fate? Did this not go against everything "development" work was striving to accomplish? Having lived in shared circumstances with the staff and students at Maria for over two years, it felt a bit like hypocrisy to leave when the going got tough.

The evacuation of expatriates coincided with my scheduled leaving date. This meant that my VSO replacement never had the opportunity to teach at Maria, and the promising group of students I had worked with for two years ended up without a qualified math teacher to see them through their GCSE. I had pushed hard to get a second grade 11 math class on the schedule, leaving twice as many Maria students affected. Across the Kavango region, countless students of expatriate teachers found themselves in similar situations. Through no fault of their own, their education was disrupted and their futures compromised. It was hard to fathom the sheer unfairness. I was angry with the circumstances, I was disappointed for my learners, and I also felt guilty for being a part of it all. I had showered my students with the usual trite platitudes about hard work paying off, but no amount of hard work would enable them to overcome obstacles over which they had no control.

LEAVING NAMIBIA

I have heard it said that the hardest part of travelling is going home, and this was certainly true for me. I returned to Canada in January 2000, but the situation in Namibia continued to preoccupy me. For months, things along the Kavango River did not improve and people continued to be maimed or killed by landmines and by soldiers. The only time the region made it into Canadian newspapers was when three children from a family of French tourists, who had apparently chosen not to heed multiple travel advisories, were killed driving along the region's main highway. This was a horrific event, but it was no worse than the deaths of so many innocent Namibians who had little choice but to be exactly where they were. Was it because the French family was white that their lives seemed more newsworthy to the Canadian media? Was it because Canadians could relate more easily to the French family than to Namibians? While I tried to figure it out, increasing numbers of Namibians were affected. Some of my former students started sleeping in the bush out of fear of an attack on the school hostel.

Even though my experiences in Namibia consumed me, they were initially very difficult to share. After over two years of living there it had become my main frame of reference for life, but I was wary of becoming one of those people who responded to anything anyone said with a "When I was in Africa …" story. While I wanted people to know about what was happening, I also knew that some of my stories would reinforce the stereotypically negative images so many people already had of Africa. I wanted people to understand that although I had thought I was going to a whole new world, I had found much of the human experience universal. I wanted people to share my new knowledge that opportunity was the only thing that was not universal.

For many reasons, I found Africa hard to stay away from. About eight months after leaving Namibia, I accepted a six-month internship in Zimbabwe, which transformed itself into a year's stay and a consultancy with the International Federation of the Red Cross. In early 2003, I returned again to work on a community development project for the Nakivale refugee settlement in southwestern Uganda. In an attempt to put all these different but valuable experiences into a wider context, I then completed a master's degree in international development.

After completing my degree, I "settled" back in Canada, unsure of when or in what capacity I would return to Africa. If I learned anything through my experiences and education, it is that Africa does not need me there. I do not possess any skills or knowledge that Africans do not have or cannot gain. I cannot justify taking a well-paid development job that in part reinforces a system I know needs to reform. Understanding the system I am a part of, I am wary of it. In many ways development workers are privileged outsiders, and I worry that for some it is the "privilege" part that sustains them. I am not sure how long I could stay true to my own beliefs and values while caught up in the larger system. At the same time, I do not think I have it in me to "do development" the way I think it should be done, over the long term and at the grassroots level.

Perhaps it is fitting, then, that when I did return to southern Africa, I went as a tourist. Almost ten years after I had first arrived, I somewhat spontaneously went back for a three-week holiday. The trip ultimately included a two-day stop in Rundu, where I stayed with an old VSO friend who had married a local Namibian woman and never left.

In many ways, it was overwhelmingly good to be back and I was happy to drink in the sights that had once made up the fabric of my daily life. Although I had a only a short time, there were a hundred places I wanted to visit and even more faces I wanted to see. But even if time had allowed, my wish was an impossible one. AIDS has taken its toll in the intervening years and with it, many familiar faces had disappeared. Among its victims was my larger-than-life former housemate, who had succumbed a few years before. It was heart rending to learn that in her final weeks, only her voice had remained strong and it had been a struggle to reconcile it with her wasted body.

I did make it out to Maria, although unfortunately my visit corresponded with school holidays and the campus was quite deserted. The school wasn't as I remembered and at first I wondered if it was just my Western eyes seeing things differently. I decided this was not the case. Maria had been a new facility when I had taught there and its continued upkeep had been a source of pride, but the broken windows and peeling paint now told a different story. It especially saddened me to see my old house in such a state of disrepair. The yard, which had always been raked to ensure that snakes would either stay away or stay visible, was now filled with weeds and garbage. The drainage canal, along the wall where my bedroom had been, oozed sewage. The last VSO to live there had recently been transferred after experiencing repeated bouts of malaria.

It was bittersweet to return to Rundu, but I am glad that I did. In retrospect I realize how angry I was when I first left Namibia. My experience up to then had allowed me the idealistic belief that the world was just. I never questioned this while living in Canada, but I suppose as a middle-class white person I never really felt the need to. Namibia forced me to look at the world in a different way. I realized my Canadian-instilled concepts of equality and justice were not being played out on the world stage. I realized that many of the opportunities I enjoyed did not come so much through any great worthiness on my part as they did from the happy coincidence of having been born white and middle class in the North. I also realized that despite grand promises, the North was not doing nearly enough to change a world order that was so obviously and fundamentally unfair for so many. I probably should have realized this long before. When I put it all together on my return from Namibia, it broke my heart.

Every day I feel blessed to have lived and worked in the developing world. I know I took far more from Africa than I gave. It is there that I experienced what I call my moments of perfect happiness, when I knew absolutely that there was nowhere else in the world I would rather be. My experiences there changed me in fundamental ways. I wish for everyone the chance to see the kinds of things I saw, for as Mark Twain wrote, "Travel is fatal to prejudice, bigotry and narrow-mindedness." Africa does not need me there, but perhaps it can use me here to share some of the things it taught me.

So now, I talk to anyone who will listen about Africa: not about tribal conflicts or starving children, and I rarely encourage people just to write a cheque or adopt a foster child. It will never be enough for us to send money to Africa out of the "goodness of our hearts." If Africa and the developing world require anything from us, it is our understanding of how absolutely intertwined our lives are and will always be. Africa can teach us to act in solidarity. Africa gives us the opportunity to act how we would want it to act should we wake up tomorrow to find the world order reversed.

Knowledge *is* power, and above all my experience in Namibia empowered me. I believe many Canadians are not more vocal about development issues simply because they do not realize that their lifestyles come at the expense of others. Namibia, and all it means to me, empowers me to encourage more Canadians to understand both the world they live in and the kinds of challenges they would face had they been born into a different part of it. I believe that when more Canadians see the world in a global context, they will choose to advocate for social justice at the local, national, and international levels. And if they are lucky, some word will come to mean to them what Namibia means to me.

3

A Night out in Malindi

Laura Madeleine Sie

Malindi is a picturesque, sleepy little town nestled on the Kenyan coast. It is a cocktail mix of African, Arabic, and South and East Asian influences that, when stirred together, result in what is known today as Swahili culture. Unlike the dry, parched regions of rural Kenya, Malindi is a haven of smouldering humidity, coastal lethargy, Swahili-style rhythms and smells, Italian expats, and colonial textures. Malindi's perpetual brightness and carefree surroundings make the town an ideal refuge from worldly troubles.

Approaching the Christmas shutdown after serving three months of our half-year volunteer assignments in Kenya's capital city of Nairobi, four fellow Canadian interns and I have chosen to spend our holidays in Malindi. The five of us have all been working on various Canadian government–sponsored development projects in Kenya and are eager to explore the coast.

Our small group of Canadian interns could be on a government poster promoting multiculturalism: it includes a multilingual Quebecker of Croatian-Austrian descent, a Toronto-suburb native of German extraction, an Ontarian born of Indonesian-Chinese immigrant parents, a third-generation Albertan–British Columbian of English origin, and an Eritrean-born Haligonian, formerly a refugee in Sudan. Perhaps it is not politically correct to describe each of our ethnic backgrounds; after all, we five are Canadian citizens in our own right, regardless of our racial origins. But race, privilege, and class affect the way we are perceived and categorized by Kenyan society and how we respond to the various situations that present themselves. As the Ontarian born of Indonesian-Chinese immigrant parents, I situate myself, not coincidentally, somewhere in the middle of the above description: I empathize with the Kenyan-born central character of MG Vassanji's 2003 Giller Prize gem, *The In-Between World of Vikram Lall*—neither former colonizer nor former colonizee in a sub-Saharan context. My physical appearance has been a source of curiosity for some local residents since my arrival in Kenya. The stares of curiosity do not occur very frequently, but when they do, that quizzical glance of amusement follows me down the streets, through the markets, and into other public spaces. I see in their facial expressions that silent question about my race hovering: "What are you?" Through my observations of the Kenyan population, it is obvious that there are very few people who look like me in Nairobi, or in all of Kenya for that matter.

As much as my ethnicity may draw unwanted attention, I sense that not having descended from the populace of a former colonial power is ultimately to my advantage. I have the feeling that the black Kenyan population perceives me as an unclassifiable, and therefore neutral and non-threatening, foreigner, a position that suits my passive personality perfectly.

Intertwined with the issue of race are questions of status and wealth. I have noted that the affluent Nairobi suburbs and satellite towns of Gigiri, Muthaiga, Parklands, Karen, and Westlands are teeming with privileged foreign expatriates and wealthy black, white, and South Asian Kenyans. But I have yet to see one single white or South Asian living in poverty, hardship, or misery. There are certainly affluent black Kenyans, but all the street kids and homeless people whom I encounter are black. I have also observed that with social status comes affluence and with affluence often comes a heightened sense of paranoia, danger, and insecurity—sentiments that seem to run rampant here in Nairobi. It appears that the gaping disparity between rich and poor plays a major role in feeding the city's high crime rate.

Our respective volunteer-sending agencies had forewarned us about the dangers and perils of "Nairobbery," a term coined by travellers and expatriates to refer to the city's crime-ridden reputation. Nevertheless, I arrived in Nairobi unprepared and blissfully ignorant of the rampant petty crime, muggings, robberies, carjackings, and beatings. A week following our arrival, walking home one night in the dark with a fellow Canadian volunteer, I learned one important rule: never walk the unlit streets of Nairobi after sundown. This I learned from a Kenyan stranger, who stopped his car alongside us, rolled down his window, and reprimanded us, two full-grown adults, for doing a "very foolish, dangerous and risky thing." He made us promise never to do it again. I never did. My fellow volunteer, however, did do it again and was violently mugged coming off a bus one evening. Out of approximately a dozen Canadian interns in Nairobi, at least four were victims of violent muggings, one suffering multiple muggings; at least two witnessed a savage beating, in one of which the victim was battered to death; one was startled from slumber one morning by the sound of a gunshot outside his bedroom window (a security guard summoned to inspect a ransacked house across the street had been gunned down in broad daylight); and another found himself at the mercy of a Kenyan police officer, who cocked a pistol at his temple after he had proved unable to produce any identification.

These incidents, and several other minor ones, have led our group to a partially justified paranoia about the "mean streets" of Kenya's urban centres. Vacationing in Malindi does not exempt us from this wariness, and we bring the apprehension that has slowly accumulated over the past three months with us to our coastal Christmas destination.

We leave three days before Christmas Day on a night bus from Nairobi to Malindi. When we were planning our vacation, several white Kenyans informed us that opting for this form of transportation was the next thing to suicide. We were warned that the night buses were notorious for getting into accidents, as the crazy, fatigued bus drivers, cranked up on amphetamines, swerved in and out of traffic in the darkness on narrow roads wedged between deep ravines. Interestingly, no black Kenyans offered such descriptions; on the contrary, they merely wished us a pleasant trip. Although we are subject to eerie, howling Swahili music blaring at full volume for the duration of our nine-hour bus ride in merciless road conditions, the bus driver is far from crazy, drugged up, or fatigued. Nor does he attempt to career in and out of traffic on the potholed roads that wind themselves around corners and bends in the never-ending obscurity. He gets us safely to Malindi ahead of schedule and without killing any of his passengers in the process.

We spend the first few hours exploring the sights, smells, tastes, and sounds of Malindi. The coastal cuisine, a savoury medley of exotic spices and local staples, is a culinary reminder of the historical Arabic and South and East Asian presence that has graced this region. The radiantly healthy complexions of the coastal people, ranging from café au lait and caramel to ebony, reflect the glittering surroundings. The fine beach sand, overhanging palm leaves, and expansive azure sky are alluring; the brilliance of the East African sun is unrelenting; the Indian Ocean is a serene and glorious turquoise. All this stands in sharp contrast, however, to the anxiety that befalls the tourists and locals after the setting of the sun.

Following a day of indulgent sunbathing, the five of us lounge at a local establishment on the main strip leading to our hostel. For all intents and purposes, the bar is "local" and we imbue it with the added benefit of being a great cultural learning experience. Our respective volunteer-sending organizations have encouraged us to frequent such establishments as a surefire way of immersing ourselves in our host country's culture and social mores. In contrast to the surrounding natural environment, however, the bar is a rather sombre affair: plastic chairs, tables, and settings; bare cement floors and walls with the odd promotional poster here and there, advertising Kenyan beers; blazing but sparse fluorescent lights casting their artificial beams on the patrons and clients. And, of course, no such establishment is complete without a radio station loudly and proudly showcasing the regional musical talent. I succumb to the hypnotic buzz of the lights, the hubbub, and the bustle of waiters skirting around the tables. After a brief scan around the bar, I note that we are the only visible foreigners here this evening.

Marija, Daniel, Eliot, Abrahet, and I are seated around the table, engaged in animated talk. I am blissfully happy, thankful for the new relationships I have forged and delighted to be in the company of likeminded individuals passionate about travel, cross-cultural exchange, and international development. As much as we are compatible in our interests and activities, we also represent diverse cultural and socioeconomic experiences—a factor that frequently leads to stimulating discussions on various issues. I sense that tonight will be another exceptional educational experience, in which personal stories and insights will be exchanged. At this point, however, I am unaware that what is about to transpire will cause me to reflect, more profoundly than ever, on issues of power, privilege, and racial hierarchy.

Of the five seated at the table, Marija has the least experience living or working in a developing country but arguably has the purest heart, the sweetest personality, and the most earnest nature. As a middle-class Quebecker of Croatian-Austrian extraction, she has dreamed of visiting Kenya for years and is delighted to be exploring parts of the country she has not yet seen. Her internship experience in Nairobi has been positive, but I sense as well that the gaping socioeconomic divide between the North and the South has in many ways broken her heart, broadened her scope, and profoundly affected her life. I suspect that her return to Canada and to all of its relative luxuries and richness will be a challenge.

Daniel is busy chattering between sips of Tusker beer. As an engineer with an acute business sense, he is an impressively persuasive and intelligent speaker. A Toronto-area native of German extraction, he has given up working on Bay Street as a corporate sales and marketing manager; he has given up pushing paper, pushing sales, pushing people, and pushing himself. He is a charming, razor-sharp young professional who might have seen his six-figure salary climb to seven if he had continued in his ways, but felt he was "turning into an asshole" and that a volunteer placement in Kenya would be good for his own salvation.

A western Canadian of English descent, Eliot is grounded, analytical, and globally aware, adept at tackling sensitive situations and assuming a role of self-effacing leadership when the need arises. He arrived in Kenya with the hope that a volunteer placement would help to clarify his career path but to date has met with nothing but disappointment. As a result of the unexpected shutdown of his local host organization, he has spent the first few months denied the opportunity to form any close personal connections. More unfortunate, he has been the victim of a violent mugging coming home after sunset one night from downtown Nairobi.

Abrahet is probably the most seasoned member of our Canadian volunteer group. The absence of immediate family members during her adolescence and an existence filled with constant challenges and struggles have made her a survivor and fighter. Although her professional objective in Kenya may be to gain work experience in an African context, her personal mission is to reunite with her Eritrean family, from whom she was separated twelve years before while living in a Sudanese refugee camp.

It is approaching 8:00 p.m. Beyond the periphery of the restaurant's lit premises, the quiet roads are veiled in shadows. As we sit, Abrahet is busy responding to an inebriated beggar, harassing us for money. She is the only one paying any attention to him. His mutterings are incoherent, his shirt and trousers are in tatters, and his wobbly swagger is gnawing at our patience. Abrahet continues to acknowledge his presence. I watch her respond politely to his inarticulate bantering as she deposits a couple of shilling coins into his outstretched hand. He does not retreat after her gesture of charity, however, but proceeds to pester the rest of us individually for a small financial donation, citing Abrahet's act of generosity to support his request. As he leans toward each of us, we recoil; he is dirty, unkempt, smelling of stale sweat and hard liquor. We four find his presence aggravating and wish that our Eritrean-born Haligonian would stop encouraging the unknown, unwelcome man.

Taking note of our uneasiness, the bar owners approach the intruder with a verbal lashing in Swahili. My Swahili is far from perfect, but I deduce from the tone that the owners are telling him to stop disturbing their prized foreign customers. I am unsure if their motives are part of an effort to keep their profits high tonight, or of an unconscious but instinctively servile reaction to please their privileged *mzungu* clients. Whatever the case, the drunkard is shooed away, much as one swats away a stray dog or cat begging for a morsel of food.

He staggers away in disappointment but leaves us with some friendly, albeit largely incoherent, parting words that our group, with the exception of Abrahet, chooses to ignore. We are thankful for his departure and dismiss the incident almost immediately, our lack of concern for his fate unmistakable. He is, after all, just another typical beggar, the kind we have encountered dozens of times in downtown Nairobi. As our conversation resumes, the jokes and stories return, and laughter is restored at our table.

There is something dream-like about the sounds and smells of the Indian Ocean waves crashing onto the shore mere footsteps away from where we are seated; the ambiance encourages free-flowing conversation and fluidity of thought.

The first warning from the bar owner does not deter the drunk from reappearing a few moments later. He eyes us, stumbles through the maze of tables and chairs, and descends upon our group for a second time. Staggering around our table, he thrusts his open palm out to each one of us in a futile plea for a few more shillings. There is a heightened aggressiveness and desperation in his requests. He becomes increasingly belligerent as we fight harder to shun him. The group, save Abrahet, ignores his demands with contempt and we shrink back in our seats with a mixture of annoyance, anxiety, and suspicion.

It isn't long before the bar staff intervenes again. They publicly humiliate him a second time for harassing the foreigners and tell him to leave the premises. With the owners hovering protectively over us, he unsteadily follows their pointing fingers directing him away from our table and out of sight, shunting him beyond the wooden fence that separates the bar from the sidewalk. He stumbles into the darkness while we resume conversation and return to our drinks. The owners are apologetic, playing the role of the concerned, protective local representatives saving face in front of their *mzungu* clients. I sense a hint of shame in their apologies, as if to dissociate themselves from the drunkard and restore the image of Malindi's residents. I observe the scene quietly and wonder if they would have provided the same attentive, apologetic service to the local clients if the beggar had approached them instead of us.

This second confrontation heightens our sense of unease, initially stirred by an incident that occurred a few hours before our arrival at the bar. While we were crossing the poorly lit road, a bare-chested man in rags had appeared abruptly, almost as an apparition, from the bushes. He was clutching a machete in each hand, much to the outward panic of Daniel and inward dread of Eliot. I barely noticed the man as he fled to the other side of the unlit street. But Daniel did: "That guy came within ten centimetres of me with a machete!" he hissed. Although isolated and random, this fleeting scene set the tone for the evening. We are suspicious of everything and are suddenly making assumptions that the drunk could actually be the man we encountered earlier on the road. The supposition is unjustified and hardly reasonable. Nevertheless, we discuss the idea of taking a taxi back to the hostel, despite being just a five-minute walk away. After all, this is nightfall in Kenya. The muggings, thefts, beatings, and shootings we witnessed in Nairobi are a constant reminder of the precautionary security measures we are often obliged to take. Not only is the road back to the hostel completely unlit, but it is also empty and winding, making us good targets for potential muggers hiding in the bushes along the way.

Despite our experiences, I cannot help but wonder if there is perhaps something racist underlying our distrust of the desperate and impoverished street people of Malindi. The fact that we have, as unpaid volunteers, the financial means to indulge in a mere two-minute taxi ride back to our hostel out of fear of being confronted by hostile thieves may seem utterly illogical outside of this context. Here in Kenya, however, all five of us acknowledge the different social situation in which we find ourselves: the experience of privilege, of being white foreigners in sub-Saharan Africa, the gaping disparity between affluence and poverty, the disturbingly high level of crime, and an omnipresent fear and paranoia. Given the context, could anyone blame us for choosing to shun this Malindi beggar, focusing instead on our own safety? I reflect that even as humanitarian volunteers, we hold the power to reject a fellow human being out of fear and self-interest. It is also ironic to me that as international development volunteers working to eliminate poverty and social exclusion in the global South, we are choosing to turn away from a man who stands to benefit the most from our work. In contemplating the incongruity between our beliefs and our actions, I realize that we have a long way to go in achieving true equality among humankind.

Ignoring the previous two warnings, the beggar resurfaces at our table for a third time. He barely has the chance to begin speaking when the bar owners descend upon him in a fit of irritation and physically remove him from the establishment. They throw him into the hands of a nearby police officer, who clubs the man over the head repeatedly with a baton. Cradling his head to shield himself from the blows, the beggar emits several pain-racked groans until his unconscious body slumps at the officer's feet.

I have my back turned to the entire beating and do not witness the attack first hand. I am, however, conscious of it as a result of the ruckus that ensues, the patrons turning to have a look and Abrahet's reaction of complete revulsion. I glance over at her; she is in a livid rage. She addresses us in incensed disbelief: "They just beat him, guys. They just beat him over the head like a wild animal. I can't fucking believe this." She stands up angrily from her chair and turns her outraged attention to the officers. "I'm going to see if he's okay."

The rupture in our group dynamic is palpable. Marija shrinks back in her chair, frightened that Abrahet would actually venture forward to see if the beggar is okay. Eliot reflects on how he will take a stand in this forthcoming dispute. I fall completely and utterly silent.

"Abrahet, you are not going anywhere. You're keeping us out of this," Daniel commands her threateningly.

She regains her seat and glares at him in outraged incredulity. "Did you not see what just happened?" she hisses, pointing her outstretched arm in the direction of the battered man. "They just beat him."

"He was harassing us, Abrahet. They told him three times to leave us alone and he didn't. He got punished for not listening."

"He's a grown man. He doesn't need to be punished like a wild animal. I'm going to see if he's all right."

"Sit down, Abrahet. Don't get us involved with the police. Don't jeopardize our safety. The guy's messed up; he's completely out of it."

Defending the battered man and challenging Daniel's don't-you-dare tone, Abrahet seethes, "He's hungry is what he is. He just wants some food to eat. He just needs a bit of money to get by. That's all he wants. He's not going to do anything to you."

The growing tension between Daniel and Abrahet troubles me more than the potential consequences of Abrahet's involvement with the beggar. I fidget in discomfort. I despise conflict. I also do not know if the apprehension I feel toward the beggar is based on legitimate fear or if it is influenced by Daniel's persuasive stance. He is an astute, well-travelled, natural-born leader. His opinion adds to my indecision. Daniel's reaction makes me worry that I have failed to see the risks we are facing. On the other hand, Abrahet's defiance is beyond her trade-mark brazenness. She is enraged and is as adamant about checking on the beggar's well-being as Daniel is resolute in keeping us out of the situation. The lines on his face betray his fear of what the local Kenyan authorities could do to us if we challenge their actions.

I turn to Marija and Eliot, who have yet to utter a single word. From their expressions, however, it is clear that self-protection is their overriding concern and that they are choosing, albeit silently, to support Daniel in this debate. Realizing that I am about to witness a very emotionally charged dialogue between three white Canadians from comfortable, privileged, middle-class backgrounds and a black Canadian who, as a former refugee, has experienced destitution and injustice first hand, I squirm.

"There are five of us here, Abrahet," Daniel asserts, "and you are the only one of us who wants to check and see if he's okay. So don't do this on our behalf. We do not want to be involved in this and we do not want to get involved with the police. You have no idea what they could do to us."

"What the hell are you scared of?" she fumes, "The man was beaten. He's lying on the ground unconscious and I just want to see if he's okay, for God's sake."

We are all silent. No one supports Abrahet. She stares in disappointment and anger at all of our disapproving faces and draws confidence from our ignorance.

"No, no," she flashes vehemently, shaking her head incredulously, her voice intensifying with every assertion. "I know I'm right, I know I am. I was a refugee and I know what this feels like. I know what this guy wants; he just wants to eat. He just wants a bit of money so he can buy some food. That's all he wants."

Daniel rebukes her angrily. "Abrahet, we are a group of foreigners and what you do to support your own opinions reflects on us as a group. We do not want to be involved in this because we do not share the same views as you."

Daniel's words continue to have a distinct influence on the emotions I am experiencing. The fear of danger seeps into me as the dispute intensifies. As much as I am uncomfortable with the tension between Abrahet and Daniel, however, I am also cognizant of the senseless violence of the beating and the underlying themes it evokes. Was the beggar beaten because the majority of us are on the top rung of a racial hierarchy? To interfere in the politics of police authority, however, is beyond what we can do. That said, I have no desire whatsoever to voice my opinion about this. And none of us want Abrahet to check and see if the man is alright. For the whites, it is a question of safety and security; for me, it is an issue of avoiding conflict. I am more concerned about interpersonal conflict than I am about the potential security threat that Abrahet's support for the beggar might bring. Daniel accuses Abrahet of misrepresenting our group, yet he doesn't realize that I do not completely share his views either. But no one knows what I think, because I am between all their views, becoming more preoccupied with my fear of conflict and confrontation as the argument deepens.

"Abrahet," Marija pleads in panic, "it's just not safe to speak to him right now. He's completely drugged up."

"Can't I just check to see if the guy is okay?" Abrahet demands angrily. "He just got clubbed in the head for God's sake."

"I just don't think that's a good idea, Abrahet." Marija continues apprehensively. "It's just not a good idea to get us involved with the police. We're foreigners; they were just trying to protect us."

"Protect us from what?" Abrahet hisses, "What was he going to do to us, anyway? Because whatever it was, it didn't deserve being clubbed in the head for it."

It is at this juncture that one of the reasons for her position surfaces: "I'm just so sick of Africans treating their own people like shit. I'm just so sick of them sucking up to white people all the time. They don't even know how to treat their own people properly."

Almost instantly the memory of a previous experience resurfaces, a seemingly trivial incident that now serves as a biting reminder of the often unspoken racial hierarchy within which the world functions. It happened one weekend when a young street boy, no more than seven years old, approached Eliot, Abrahet, and me while we were strolling along Mama Ngina Street in downtown Nairobi. As I listen to Abrahet's condemnation of this racial hierarchy, I wonder if the boy was too young to realize the pecking order with which he had solicited the three of us for money: the white first, the Asian second, and the black last. Of the three Canadian volunteers he approached, it was the black who placed a few shilling coins onto the boy's outstretched palm.

Abrahet shakes her head in anger and disbelief. "You guys don't even look at these people as humans. These are people, for fuck's sake. These are human beings."

"Abrahet, we know these people are human beings." Marija's hurt, wide-eyed expression is gently indignant. Her humanitarian heart is getting the better of her.

"Then why didn't any of you talk to that man who tried to help us when we got off the bus at the station this morning?" Abrahet demands.

I have to remind myself what she is referring to. That morning, as we got off the bus, a man had approached us, eager to show us to our hostel. We were all aware of the trick: the stranger would feign a show of hospitality and warm welcome, engage us in friendly conversation, bring us to our hotel door, and then demand money. It has happened countless times already and we have been annoyed at being offered falsely friendly conversations only to be sworn at later for failing to provide any monetary reward for the "voluntary" escort. The unfortunate guide awaiting our arrival this morning was dismissed and ignored from the minute he approached us.

"We don't need any assistance, thank you," said Eliot politely. "We know where we're going."

But as the ploy goes, the man assured us that he knew a short cut and could get us there in half the time. We rolled our eyes, avoiding eye contact and any conversation starters. He followed us down the curving roads and sandy alleyways until we found ourselves at the doors of our hostel entrance. By this time, he had given up on everyone save Abrahet, the only one who had not ignored him. When we arrived at the hostel, he advanced his open palm in the all-too-familiar gesture for money. While the four of us turned our backs to him, Abrahet opened up her wallet and deposited twenty shillings into his callused hand. As he walked away, I looked pensively after him and wondered whether or not he was happy with his new fortune, the equivalent of approximately forty Canadian cents.

"Did any of you talk to the man who walked with us to the hostel?" Abrahet demands.

"Did you talk to him?" she confronts Eliot, who is still silently reflecting on how he will respond to the issue at hand.

"Did you talk to him?" she shifts her attention to Daniel. He is too incensed and concerned for the group's safety to answer her.

"Did you talk to him?" she turns to Marija, who is too shell-shocked by this feisty and uncompromising version of our usually friendly and jovial Abrahet to provide a response.

"Did you talk to him?" she stares pointedly at me. Her accusatory words are piercing.

"No, I did not," I mutter shamefacedly. It is the only verbal contribution that I will make during this entire altercation.

"Not a single one of you acknowledged his presence. Not one." She challenges our gazes with a squarely focused stare. I fidget uncomfortably. "I was the only one who talked to him. I was the only one who paid him any money after he walked all the way with us to the hostel from the bus station."

"But Abrahet, why would I want to befriend someone who clearly only wants to be friendly with me for money?" Eliot asks calmly.

"Why do you have to look at it that way?" she persists defiantly. "He just wanted to make an honest penny. Was it that horrible to give him twenty shillings for walking with us from the bus station? That's forty cents for God's sake."

"But they were services that we clearly didn't need, Abrahet." His tone and voice are devoid of any form of aggressiveness. "We knew how to get to the hostel ourselves. Why should we have paid for a service we didn't want?"

Abrahet continues, "None of you even talked to him, or even acknowledged his presence. It's just about simple respect for a fellow human being. That's all. And you couldn't even give him that."

"But can you understand why I might be suspicious of people randomly looking for money?" Eliot continues patiently. "I was robbed and choked to unconsciousness a few weeks ago. Don't you think that would make me less likely to trust a stranger?"

His mugging has affected Eliot deeply. Only a few short weeks ago he was violently assaulted one evening in the darkness while making an ill-timed bus transfer in a dangerous part of downtown Nairobi. Although the streets were littered with people, a group of black men grabbed him about the throat, choked him to unconsciousness, and robbed him of his money and belongings. No one stopped to help. After they had stripped him of his glasses and abandoned his unconscious body on the street, Eliot regained awareness and then struggled blindly with his hands to find a taxi that finally brought him safely home. Despite experiencing some discomfort the following day, he recovered physically. The same cannot be said however, about his emotional state. Eliot is now distrustful of those he subconsciously judges to be "dubious" or "questionable-looking" black Kenyans. It is a lamentable consequence of the assault and I have witnessed the apprehension he feels first hand. While walking home a couple of weeks following the mugging, Eliot and I noted in the distance a black Kenyan man walking briskly toward us. He did not have the appearance of a beggar or street person, but I immediately sensed Eliot's discomfort and distrust. He nudged me gently in the waist and uttered a soft but panicked "Let's cross the road now." We did so in plain view of the approaching man, most likely utterly offended by our blatant act of suspicion toward him. It is actions such as this one that underline the prejudiced and preconceived fear and apprehension that Abrahet is now condemning him for.

"You can't judge everyone like that," she retorts in anger. "You just happened to meet this one group of bad men on the streets of Nairobi and now you're assuming that everyone else who's black and poor is out to get you."

Unlike Abrahet, the rest of us are more concerned for our own safety than we are about this beating or the racial inequality it illustrates. In awkward dismay, I observe the growing racial divide between the three white people and the one black person engaged in this debate. Even more alarming is that three of the group have now united against the only black member, leaving her to defend herself and her convictions. I observe this racial imbalance and am torn between wanting to stand in solidarity with a fellow Canadian of colour and fearing an unknown, intoxicated man, as well as a group of Kenyan police. I also cannot help but feel resentment toward the three privileged white Canadians who, in my eyes, completely fail to understand why Abrahet is reacting so angrily to this man's beating. The feeling stems from my personal experiences growing up as an Asian in a predominantly white society, sometimes feeling underprivileged or inferior on various levels as a result of my ethnicity. But my resentment also stems from my own unfair assumption that the whites have never personally experienced these feelings of inferiority, marginalization, or race-based discrimination and are consequently too fortunate to see beyond their own concerns and fully comprehend the injustice of this situation and the idea of racial superiority it evokes. Ultimately, however, in my characteristic nature of not wanting to offend anyone, I don't take sides but leave my perspective of the situation unsaid.

I reflect upon how stereotypically "Asian" it is of me to sit mutely on the fence in an effort to avoid conflict and confrontation. It strikes me at this point that our responses to the incident appear to be race based. Perhaps it is not as cut and dried as the following, but what I observe is this. The whites are fearful of the destitute, inebriated African man as well as of the Kenyan authorities. The black is challenging us not to found our fears on preconceived stereotypes about poverty and security but to regard the man as an individual human being worthy of dignity, humanity, and respect. The Asian is mutely and awkwardly occupying no man's land, distressed about the ill feelings that accompany conflict. Only Abrahet empathizes with the beggar's situation. She sees his situation through the eyes of a former refugee living in hardship, and as a woman of African descent she recognizes this act of violence as an injustice that many fellow blacks experience. The fear of getting involved is one thing, but I wonder whether our decision to turn our backs on the beggar masks something deeper. Perhaps as non-black bystanders, we can choose to ignore the incident because we have no personal stake and cannot identify with it as Abrahet does.

Finally, Abrahet gets up out of her seat for good. "I'm sorry, guys," she mutters unapologetically, disappointed and angry with our no-show of support. "I don't care if you all disagree with me because I know I'm right about this. I know I am." She defiantly leaves our table to check on the man's well-being.

"Abrahet, don't," Daniel starts angrily.

But it is too late. She has already made her way to the beaten man and the group of police officers surrounding him.

Daniel, Eliot, and Marija resign themselves to the fact that trouble and danger now lie before us. Their reaction heightens my own anxiety; I fret about the unbearable dissonance that will result from this ordeal. It disturbs me that only hours ago, we were five friends interacting warmly and jovially with one another, unconcerned with any racial differences. Although the conflict among us is my utmost concern, my easily swayed personality, coupled with everyone's frantic response to Abrahet's decision, leads me to believe that something horribly frightening will now follow.

"I can't believe she's doing this," mutters Daniel between nervous gulps of beer. "None of us here want to be involved in this."

I consciously keep my back turned to the affair that ensues, out of both desire to remain at a distance and fear of witnessing further violence. Abrahet approaches the beaten man to see if he has regained consciousness and offers him some words of concern and support. She then turns her outraged energy to the police officers and verbally castigates them for their inhumane treatment of a fellow African. This is the final straw for Daniel. When she returns to our table, he is in a state of nervous fury.

"We are all leaving now, Abrahet and you are coming with us," he commands. Our bills are paid with lightning speed and our table is cleared in seconds. The tension has reached its climax.

With no taxi in sight, we begin the longest five-minute walk in the dark any of us have ever known. The beaten man has regained consciousness and attaches himself to Abrahet, accompanying us back to our hostel. Eliot, in a gesture of masculine duty, instructs Marija and me to walk ahead so that he and Daniel can serve as a buffer zone between the man and the two non-black women. I instinctively fold my hands into two fists in an act of preparatory self-defence as I watch Marija speed on into the darkness. Although I can hear Abrahet in the background chattering openly with the man, I detect an element of discomfort in her voice as she comes to the realization that he is pursuing us back to our hostel. The road is cloaked in darkness. The only sounds we register are the rhythmic thumps of our hurried footsteps and the chiming of Abrahet's uneasy laughter. The voice of the beaten man is barely audible, his purpose and intentions completely unknown to us. We have put a sizeable distance between him and the four of us, the two Canadian males glancing backward frequently to keep watchful tabs on Abrahet. Images of the man's partners in crime descending violently upon us along the winding road chase me back to our hostel. Not until we reach the hostel's lit porch do I realize that my clenched fists are aching and damp.

But in the end, no one is harmed, no one physically threatened. After refusing his requests for more money, Abrahet instructs the man to leave and return home. "I already gave you some," she says firmly. "No more." He retreats into the darkness as we climb the stairs of our two-star hostel.

Once in our rooms, the tension that I have dreaded is blatantly apparent. Relieved yet enraged, Daniel announces that he is retiring for the night and leaves. Eliot, Marija, Abrahet, and I remain. I have yet to utter a word of worth since the entire affair began and I am still reflecting pensively on the night's event, unsure of what to say in the nervous silence that follows. In the end it is Abrahet who speaks up first.

"Guys, I'm sorry if this got personal and I apologize for that," she starts gently, "but I just feel very strongly about this and I want you all to understand why it is I reacted this way. I was a refugee; I know what it's like to be in that guy's position. I know what it's like to be hungry, desperate, and shunned. I know what it feels like."

Abrahet halts momentarily before addressing the underlying reason for her wrath. "It frustrates me to see Africans treating their own people so badly. I hate watching them suck up to whites all the time. It's demeaning and they make themselves feel inferior. I'm sorry for making this personal or attacking you personally, but I really do feel that I'm right about everything else."

What follows is an inconclusive recapitulation of the event and a brief but less emotionally charged conversation about the issues that arose. Fatigue sets in. Abrahet and Marija get up and announce that they are turning in for the night, leaving Eliot and me to discuss the situation in private.

"I'm impressed with how you dealt with the situation," I say admiringly. "You brought up some good points."

He shrugs off the comment, as if unaware that I am offering him a compliment. As an afterthought, Eliot replies meditatively, "I sort of enjoy these opportunities to discuss differences of opinions and to mediate conflict. It's very enriching."

I marvel at the beauty of his words, all the more so because my default approach to conflict resolution is to avoid the conflict.

Reflecting on this incident two years later, I am surprised at the idea that our responses to the incident could be divided by race: were we not all Canadian, sharing the same values, education, opportunities, and privileges? No, we were not. Abrahet had had very different experiences from the rest of us. For me, as a non-white Canadian, the situation drove home the influence of all the stereotypes, prejudices, and cultural assumptions associated with my skin colour—influences that ultimately determined my silence.

Now that I live in a relatively safe and secure environment, in familiar territory back in Canada and not exposed to the abject poverty I witnessed in Kenya, it is much easier for me to regret my mute response to the beating. But I am nevertheless disappointed that we, a group of globally minded Canadians and international development workers at that, did not support Abrahet's concern about the beggar's well-being, even after she pointed out his destitution and our tendency to respond out of fear and prejudice. We were looking for opportunities to "make the world a more just and equitable place," but when confronted with the chance to care for the beaten man, we were unable to muster enough compassion. We preach philosophies of promoting equality and eliminating injustice, but our rejection of the Malindi beggar may well be an indication that well-intentioned beliefs do not translate into day-to-day actions.

Back in Canada, I see the Malindi beggar in the homeless Canadians I encounter on the streets every day. For the first time in my life, I do not feel fear or discomfort, or turn away when I hear their requests. I do not give anything—this has never been my way of attempting to find a personal solution to the poverty I confront either in Canada or elsewhere—but I take a moment to acknowledge the other's presence out of respect and recognition for a fellow human. I am sensitive to the socio-economic divide between us and realize that even for a person of colour, privilege comes in many forms. Although I may have felt deprived of certain advantages throughout my life as a visible minority in a predominantly white population, I recognize my good fortune as a healthy, educated, middle-class Canadian to whom choices and opportunities are abundantly available.

For me, the beating of the Malindi beggar is a poignant reminder of the unspoken social and racial hierarchy that the world continues to accept, and of the power struggles that ensue. Everything took on a different political and cultural meaning in Kenya: a bus ride, a stroll down the street, an encounter with a beggar, the choice of vacation destination, personal safety and security. Every interaction was loaded with the weight of colonial history and the precedent of racial exclusion. Every action we took contributed, either positively or negatively, to the dialogue on race in a postcolonial world. Experiences like these compel me to reflect continuously on the decisions I make as a Canadian working in the field of international development.

Ultimately, it is not merely financial aid and the development of strong economies that will reduce the divide between the global North and the global South. Rather, progress toward global justice and equality requires us to redress simultaneously hierarchical perceptions of race and culture and the inequities they perpetuate. We are trained as development workers to build capacity, strive toward sustainability, and empower underprivileged communities. Yet in my experience, we still have a lot to learn about how we view the disadvantaged: not as potential security threats or as recipients of pity and paternalism but as fellow humans seeking a better life for themselves and the generations to come.

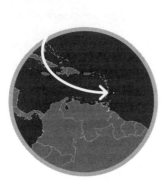

4

No Man Is an Island

Lessons in Interdependence Learned
in Barbados

Alika Hendricks

> Never doubt that a small group of thought-
> ful, committed people can change the world.
> Indeed, it is the only thing that ever has.
> —*Margaret Mead*

My father has been known to impart little nuggets of
wisdom from time to time. They vary in their degree of
applicability, and some are plainly contestable, but there
is one that I have come to believe is true. Should I take it
to heart, I have no doubt that it will take me far in life.
"Pooks," he says, "Life is about relationships. It's all about
relationships." When I reflect on my time as a student in
Barbados, I realize that relationships of all kinds and at
all levels are where things *happen*. Relationships bring
people together, and when people come together dreams
are realized. Some might call it networking, but perhaps
the term is too cold to describe the process that I saw
unfold on that warm Caribbean island.

Nearing the end of my degree in international
development studies, it was clear to me that without any
hands-on experience my world knowledge was useless,

my competence a farce. I had crossed the globe dozens of times, conversed with the economically impoverished of many nations—all in the comfort of my own room, while turning the pages of my textbooks. When the prospect of studying abroad as part of a field study semester presented itself, I leapt at the chance. Not only would the program enable me to narrow my focus and concentrate on one geographical area (Barbados) and one development problem (water resource management), but it also included an internship component, a long-awaited opportunity to apply all that I had been learning.

The program emphasized an interdisciplinary approach to development, specifically water resource management. We were therefore an academically diverse group, specializing in subjects as disparate as chemical engineering and geography. The purpose was to tap into the synergy of our varied experiences. The program coursework also reflected our diversity, and it was assumed that each of us would at some point function outside of our academic comfort zones. For me, moments of unfamiliarity were to be the norm. As one of the few social science students in the program, I found that hydrology, irrigation, and the many manifestations of wastewater posed entirely new (and unsettling) challenges.

The story would probably end here had the program been nothing more than classes and homework in a tropical setting. Fortunately, however, my studies abroad were to extend beyond the classroom, thanks to the mandatory internship component in sustainable development planning.

The challenge of finding a suitable host organization soon became evident to my teammates, Andrea and Raquel, and me. We needed an organization to accommodate the three of us, two days a week, for the entire semester. It was a big commitment to ask anyone to take on but we thought, perhaps naïvely, we had plenty to give. The three of us possessed remarkably different skills: Andrea was an agro-environmental engineering student and Raquel a natural scientist with a penchant for domesticated animals. I had the dubious role of development theory specialist. Our first mission was to find a host and mutually determine what needs we, as interns, could reasonably meet that would also fulfil the requirements of our sustainable development term project. The task was not a simple one.

While a list of potential internship hosts had been compiled prior to our arrival in Barbados, finding a *good* match took a great deal of additional effort. The expectations of some prospective hosts were too high: "Design a wastewater-reusing irrigation system for our community." In other cases, they were entirely too vague: "Well, what are *you* interested in doing for *us*?" Stuck and frustrated, my teammates and I departed from the prepared list of options and stumbled upon an interesting article in the national newspaper, the *Barbados Advocate*.

Nestled in the middle of the paper was an unusual headline that read, "Disabled helping to boost organic agriculture." The article went on to describe a project being proposed by the Organic Growers and Consumers Association (OGCA) to the Canadian International Development Agency. It spoke of building "personal pride and self-worth" while tackling the "pressing issue of national food security." We were intrigued. Andrea, decided to track down the man interviewed in the article, Philip Gibbs, the secretary of the OGCA. From what we read in the newspaper, this association could potentially be a good internship host. Furthermore, organic farming was an area that my co-interns were especially interested in. The next step would be to convince the association that they would benefit from having three novices in their midst for four months.

We soon found out that the OGCA was little more than a fledgling group of Barbadian organic farmers—but with an inspiring vision to expand organic farming across the country and throughout the Caribbean. It was a vision that my partners and I wanted to be a part of. How were we to convince these farmers that we would be more of a benefit to them than a burden?

As luck would have it, we had very little convincing to do. We were welcomed with open arms, as green as we were. Our new hosts encouraged us to let go of our insecurities. It was to be a learning process for all of us. Enthusiasm and a positive outlook were all that they required.

My first encounter with Philip, our new internship host, was also a first meeting (one of many) with his much-loved and very worn out white pickup truck. The truck was like Philip's sidekick: a stalwart friend and supporter that was always there, and always good for a laugh, especially when it sputtered, moaned, or needed a boost. Into the cab of this ramshackle vehicle my internship partners and I were ushered for our first meeting with Philip.

Once I had settled into a seat in the front, a cup of thick, greenish liquid was thrust through the window into my hand by a man seated in the back of the truck. I was told it was golden apple juice, made from a hard, elliptical fruit that looked nothing like the apples I knew. Hesitant but trying to make a good first impression, I sipped the unknown liquid—and found it to be surprisingly and reassuringly sweet. This odd yet pleasant start to our first meeting was to set the tone for our semester spent alongside Philip and the many other farmers and friends we were to meet.

We talked as we drove along in the truck. The conversation meandered, much like the winding Barbadian back roads that took us from our campus to Philip's farm. He asked about our studies and our feelings about Barbados. Eventually the conversation swung around to agriculture and the project at hand.

Aside from his involvement with the OGCA, Philip was in the process of developing a new project in collaboration with a handful of small-scale organic farmers from across the country. *This* was the project that he wanted our help with. We would not be working for the OGCA after all, but rather with Philip and a somewhat amorphous amalgam of farmers collaborating on a specific organic farming expansion project. My co-interns and I realized that we would be witnessing a significant step forward for agriculture in Barbados and the wider Caribbean: collective farming and organic agriculture.

This new collective was called the Bath Organic Cultural Farm (BOCF). It aimed to bring together several small-scale farmers to cultivate a substantial parcel of land using organic farming practices. The guiding principle was to promote the "holistic management and sustainable development" of seventy-three acres of land at Bath Plantation in the Parish of St. John, Barbados, a dazzlingly lush area of sloping terrain overlooking the Atlantic Ocean. Though not at all large by the standards of industrialized agriculture, this would be the largest plot of land to be designated for organic farming in the country. For its visionaries, Bath symbolized the fruition of big hopes to promote food security on the island, which had long been a sugarcane mono-crop agricultural sector. As interns, our mandate was to promote sustainable development. Working with an organic farming collective seeking to diversify away from the ailing sugar sector was a great opportunity for us.

Philip believed strongly in learning by doing. He was of the opinion that if we interns were to learn about organic farming in Barbados, it would be done with a shovel in our hands, not through a literature review. Ultimately, though, we used both. When I was not out in the fields at Philip's farm, I was studying the pros and cons of farming collectives and, based on my findings, I developed a human resource plan for the project. It was to be a sort of "collective framework," outlining ways to minimize the challenges and maximize the advantages of collective farming.

The more I studied, the more I realized how few practical resources there were. I needed answers, but theoretical, academic resources were getting me only so far. It was time, I decided, to consult a genuine expert in the field of development. I made a call to social analyst Schofield Fredericton at the Caribbean Development Bank. He was quick to share his reservations. "Collective farming, you say? That kind of thing just doesn't work in Barbados." I assured him that there was a group of organic farmers who thought differently, and asked for his advice. He encouraged me to organize focus groups to get the participating farmers talking about what they hoped to get out of the collective, about their concerns and also what they thought they brought to the project. "Most importantly," he said, "try to find out if everyone is on the same page." In his experience, interpersonal dynamics could make or break a group like the one I described. I took Schofield's advice seriously.

Even the irrepressibly optimistic Philip had mentioned that personal differences sometimes flared.

The collective framework would not only help to identify and resolve conflict among the farmers but would also form part of the BOCF's official proposal to the government's Land for the Landless Programme. This would allow the program to officially acquire the land at Bath Plantation, which had once been home to one of the island's original sugar estates. In its colonial days, the majestic plantation house, flanked with grand porches, had looked out over the Atlantic. The property had also featured an outdoor bath house, from which the plantation took its name. The small stone structure that was once a place of rest and relaxation for the sugar plantation's owners was still there, and a natural spring still fed into it. The crystal clear spring had been given new life in recent times as a favourite bathing spot for members of the Rastafarian community located nearby. The water of the spring was coveted for its purity: free from government-added chemicals like fluoride.

Those who lived in the immediate environs knew the plantation well. They had seen it change hands a number of times and then lie fallow. Finally, the government designated it part of its Land for the Landless Programme, with the intention that the plantation be transferred back into the hands of those who could make good use of it. Philip and his farming friends at the BOCF aimed to fill this role. They also hoped to incite social change by enticing young people from the surrounding area to join the collective. The hope was that the young would once again take an interest in the land, instead of forsaking it for city life.

There is nothing quite like manual work to stimulate profound conversation. My body got into the rhythm of its task until it became almost automatic, and then my mind was released to focus elsewhere. I came to understand that the most important learning is likely to be born out of ordinary conversations and moments of perspective-gaining silence. Out on the farm, working in the open air, it was clear to me why the farmers had such a love for the land. Working the land brought them together and allowed for the airing of life's real issues. All topics were fair game: ethics, politics, love, loss. They spoke with openness and honesty about themselves. They shared their feelings about their families, and about their faith.

One hot and sticky morning, Andrea, Raquel, and I were helping with the mulching. We talked as we worked and somehow the conversation turned to the eternal: what happens when we die. Raquel asked, "Do you think there is anything after this life?" Our hoes dug into the soil, turning over earth before digging in again.

"Like reincarnation?" asked Andrea.

"Yeah, maybe," answered Raquel, "or heaven." We could hear our breathing. The air was thick, heavy with heat and our thoughts.

It was a question I had been working on too, turning it over and over in my head. My closest aunt had died two days before my departure for Barbados. Finally I said, "Heaven is a place you believe in when you have to. When people you love die, it's the only conviction that gives hope. I have to believe my Aunty is there." Sweaty, squatting in the dirt, I felt close to them in that moment. Our souls were being unearthed. We were engaged in a very tangible task, but the intangible was there with us. Perhaps agriculture reminds us of the small mysteries—like that of making a seed grow—and reminds us too that there are many other mysteries worth considering.

In each of our farmer friends, I found a life lesson. I learned about quiet leadership. Ian, for example, was a farmer of very few words, every one just what he meant to say and just what was needed at that time: "Remember to listen" and "Be grateful always." I was moved by his gentleness and honesty.

Marvin, Philip's young protégé, took us fishing and shared stories about his life, the mistakes he'd made, and his gratitude for the present: "Today is a new day, right? A new, new day. So what are we going to do?" At the market on Saturday mornings I witnessed the power of patience and generosity. Each hand-picked item—tomato, thyme, yam, hot pepper— lovingly passed from a farmer's hands to the hands of an expectant customer. For Philip and the other farmers, each transaction was an act of realizing the hope of a new and healthier Barbadian agricultural sector.

Through our discussions, I gained insight into their appreciation for nature and the interconnectedness of humanity and the environment. "Food grounds us," they said, "and gives a sense of place." It would be a cultural farm indeed, a farm to counter the dominant culture of store-bought food in which farmer and consumer live worlds apart. It would celebrate the connection between people and the earth.

For our Rastafarian friends, spiritual and physical health were intrinsically linked. So were politics and pollutants. They sought to distance themselves from "the establishment" and live off the land. Some of the farmers achieved this ideal; others were working toward it. Either way, organic farming was a natural extension of these aspirations. Pesticides were in direct opposition to their philosophy of all-natural goodness.

To them, natural was not only good—it was the best. They were passionate about sharing this ideal with others and eagerly discussed the importance of good food and health consciousness with their customers at the market. In fact, despite the high prices that organic foods generally fetched because of their labour-intensive and specialized cultivation, the farmers we worked with sold their goods at the market prices charged for conventional produce. They did it to encourage consumers to buy organic: "to ease them into it," they said. They wanted customers to discover the difference for themselves. It worked, too. Week after week, I observed many of the same customers at the market lining up by the organic stall.

The benefits of organic farming to both human and environmental health were becoming increasingly well known the world over. However, as I would soon find out, farming without chemical pesticides or herbicides comes at a cost: weeding, mulching, and other labour-intensive tasks pose a substantially larger burden for organic farms than for conventional farms. For this reason, the farmers considered community involvement essential to organic agriculture. If more than a few acres of land were to be cultivated, the community had to work together, sharing labour, expertise, equipment, and marketing capacity.

Unfortunately, as Schofield had warned, the concept of working together for mutual gain had earned a very poor reputation in much of the Caribbean. As my research continued to reveal, agricultural collectives in particular had a dismal track record. In the 1960s and 1970s, co-operatives had spread throughout the Caribbean. They were considered to be an ideal way of empowering small-scale farmers. For a number of reasons though, many of these schemes ultimately failed. A poor incentive system with meagre and slow-turning profits eroded morale. Theft or attempts to circumvent equitable profit sharing thwarted success. Poor management undermined collective efforts. Or sometimes, as Schofield had warned, personality clashes were to blame. There were challenges at the macro-economic level as well, with increasingly conservative government policies and a geopolitical climate that promoted privatization and "agricultural modernization" as the keys to progress.

The collective framework I designed was meant to address these multifarious issues. It tackled the points of contention most likely to arise, outlined conflict resolution strategies, and made suggestions for task delegation. Still I wondered if it was enough. Perhaps co-operation went against our innately selfish human nature. I was disturbed by my scepticism, and yet the burden of proof was not in favour of believing otherwise.

Four collaborating farms were intended to make up the collective at Bath: Pot House Organic and Cultural Group, Bawden Environmental Park Group, Kornerstone Organic Farms, and the Ichirouga-naim Council for the Advancement of Rastafari. Three of the four were explicitly Rastafarian groups. There was no Rastafarian prerequisite for involvement in the collective, and in fact Philip, our primary contact, was not Rastafarian. Nevertheless, it was this Rastafarian bent that led to the inclusion of the word *cultural* in the name of the project at Bath. Each of the farms operated according to its own norms and its own interpretation of Rastafarian doctrine. Rastafarianism has a number of denominations, each with distinct practices and beliefs. As in any other religious community, these differences were sometimes divisive.

The Bath project was meant to be an opportunity to overcome differences and focus on a theme that unified the groups: organic agriculture. The mandate was not religious in any sense, and yet it was at the sticky site of interdenominationalism that conflict arose, most unexpectedly one afternoon after a wonderful day spent at Eden.

Eden was the name of a farm affiliated with Bawden Environmental Park. It was a lush place, lovingly owned and operated by Robert Alleyne, the acting president of the OGCA. After spending a day with him, Andrea, Raquel, and I were to attend one of the association's meetings, where I would have a chance to talk one on one with some of the members who were also to be involved with the Bath collective.

It was just before dusk and we were the first to arrive at the meeting. By this time, my co-interns and I had become accustomed to the flexible approach to punctuality taken by many Barbadians, but on this particular occasion it seemed that something was amiss. We could not have known then that the sombre mood of evening would serve as a fitting backdrop to the unpleasant scene that would unfold.

We waited a long time. Eventually, a husband-and-wife team from the Ichirouganaim group pulled up and got out of their car. Robert spoke out a word of greeting to them in the semi-darkness. They did not respond warmly. They had been wronged and had come to inform the president of the association that they were dissatisfied with the way that things were being run. What was more, they felt they had been personally slighted. It was never entirely clear to me what the problem was. What was clear was that the boundary of amicable business relations had been crossed and we were into the much more volatile territory of personal hurt.

On that evening, I processed little of what was said. I was too awestruck and disappointed. Angry words were spoken. People's religious convictions were haughtily challenged. Names were called. One questioned, "Are women to be included?" The other asked, "Who will really be in charge?" And finally, "We don't plan to work just to advance someone else's agenda." The association meeting never took place. No one else turned up—an inauspicious sign. Were the disgruntled couple emissaries of others who also harboured suspicions about the project? It was not clear. But the initial focus group meeting that I had put together to mine for traces of potential conflict never took place. Unfortunately, I did not have another opportunity to discuss the Bath project with the full body of the association's members.

It was a sobering reality check for me. If individual, divisive opinions could not be put aside for a common purpose, then the project, I feared, was doomed. While Robert had handled the situation with utmost grace and patience, the result was the same. It was a setback for everyone. The incident revealed, I feared, an underlying lack of trust and lightly veiled hostility between some of the people who were to be members of the collective. Until that moment, it had all seemed so feasible—it was only a matter of working out the logistics. Suddenly, logistical details seemed to be the least significant thing to overcome.

Though the possibility of interpersonal conflict was to be an omnipresent dark cloud for me, it was compensated for by the radiant goodness of the individual farmers who gave their time and space to ensure that we interns felt useful and appreciated. The internal relationship challenges were also offset by fortuitous interactions with people and organizations from the outside, whose support would be integral to manifesting the vision.

It became clear that the ability to build and make use of relationships would be essential to ensure that the Bath Organic Cultural Farm would be selected for the Land for the Landless Programme. For me, the manoeuvrings that took place to this end were a first look at the immense power of building networks and drumming up support. Agencies and organizations of all kinds (local, national, multinational) were looking to support projects that appeared destined for success. I soon learned that to secure the necessary backing, word about the project had to be in circulation—and this Philip executed masterfully.

Philip invited my partners and me to attend a tour of his farm that he was hosting for representatives from the United Nations

Development Programme (UNDP) Global Environment Facility (GEF), among others. The tour itself related to a personal project of his, but he thought it would be useful for us to attend. He picked us up from our residence and drove us out to the farm, where we arrived not long before the expected guests.

They pulled up alongside Philip's battered old truck in sports utility vehicles. Decked out in high-heeled pumps and business suits, they seemed unprepared for a farm tour of any variety, much less on a sticky day like that one. Toting notebooks, clipboards, and cellphones, the very official development personnel were led around the grounds. Farming being what it was, there was not much to see at that particular time of year. No impressive crops were growing, nor had any bountiful display been set up to welcome the guests. Rather Philip spun gold with his dream-laden words. He described what had been and what was. He then painted a mental picture of what could be ... with the generous support of our well-dressed friends.

It is impossible for me to say just what was meant to come out of that farm tour. I suppose it was an opportunity for the various representatives to see where their development dollars had gone, and perhaps to ensure continued support for Philip's farm. But when people are together, they get to talking and sometimes they talk about things not quite relevant to the issue at hand. It was in this way that my co-interns and I got to talking with one of the UNDP representatives about the Bath collective project. He took the bait—and we took his card.

Stanford Ellis, the UNDP GEF representative, was a large man of imposing stature, but ever so good to talk to. He was in the business of providing start-up capital to promising agricultural initiatives, and he seemed to know a good project when he saw one. Only a few short weeks after we met him at Philip's farm, he summoned us for a meeting at UNDP headquarters to discuss the Bath collective project further. It was evident that Raquel, Andrea, and I had been invited out of courtesy. The real work of hammering out a plan was strictly between the collaborating farmers and Stanford.

The project had not yet even been granted the land, and already discussions were being held about how to fund the largely hypothetical venture. It was an amazing sight to behold. Clearly a huge element of faith was involved. Philip was so convinced of the project's viability that the normal order of events was gleefully abandoned in favour of securing any and all possible support. I slowly came to see that Philip was on the right track. There was little chance that the government would say no to the Bath collective's proposal for the land if the project had already secured UNDP support.

The government agency charged with selecting the most worthy applicants for entry into the Land for the Landless Programme was the Barbados Agricultural Development and Marketing Corporation (BADMC). The BADMC would decide the fate of the plantation at Bath, and by extension, the fate of the Bath collective project. An article in the *Barbados Advocate* suggested that though nothing was official, the agency itself considered the BOCF to be an excellent candidate. "Bath Plantation is being looked at exclusively as an organic area," Mr. Harrison of the BADMC was reported as saying. Further, it was mentioned that the BADMC hoped to encourage a "co-operative movement" to manage the land. However, no formal approval had been granted.

The newspaper article outlined the intention of BADMC to set up a new irrigation system on the plantation site before the land would be available for occupancy. This was an exciting piece of news for our internship group since Andrea, the agro-engineering student, had the skills to design the necessary irrigation system. We placed a call to Mr. Harrison.

Our first meeting with him was dizzying. Numbers and technical terminology were flung at us. He dodged our questions and enumerated a list of demands. Due to a personnel shortage, he was without an engineer. He needed one. The negotiating process involved give and take, push and pull, in the aim of finding a position that both sides could handle.

Finally Mr. Harrison said that if Andrea thought she could handle it, she could take on the task of creating an appropriate irrigation system design. Andrea agreed to design the system (for free, no less) on the condition that her plan be allowed to conform to organic farming standards. He was willing to accept that condition. Almost seamlessly, another step was taken toward ensuring that the collective would be an irrefutable candidate for the land at Bath Plantation.

As the semester drew to a close, reports were written up and final presentations given. Andrea, Raquel, and I passed over our project deliverables: an irrigation design, a collective farming framework, and a livestock care guide. Our efforts were a stack of paper. I felt cheated and a bit apprehensive. How was it all going to come together? Would the conflicts be resolved? And if it did work out, the best was yet to come and we wouldn't be there to see it. It was Andrea who said, "We don't always get to see things through to the end. Sometimes we must just trust that they have been left in good hands."

Barbados was indeed a small island. There was a distinctly small-town feel to the place and it was charming, for a time at least. Even a quick trip to the grocery store had been punctuated with waves, nods, smiles, and shouted hellos. Some would say anonymity was impossible. But even the small society of just over 250,000 people had its own subcultures, and the Rastafarian farming community was one of these. Through my involvement with the Bath Organic Cultural Farm collective, I had got a unique glimpse into that tightly knit community. Moreover, I had had the opportunity to share in their struggles and to help lay the groundwork for expected successes.

A few months after I left Barbados, my semester having come to an end, I discovered that the BOCF had been awarded the grant of land at Bath Plantation. Andrea, Raquel, and I were proud to have played a role in that process. Ours were just a few of the many hands to have held and coddled the project that started as an idea and grew into a shared vision before taking its mature, concrete form.

I did not go to Barbados expecting to appreciate the importance of learning how to collaborate with people in order to reach a shared dream, but learning about relationships is ultimately what I have taken with me. Relationships can be the greatest vehicles to obtaining desired outcomes—but gone sour, they can also be the greatest obstacles to achieving success.

My time spent with those hardworking farmers was also extremely humbling. I was reminded that even the best help I could provide would ultimately not decide the future of their project. The farmers themselves were their own best advocates. They alone understood the relational nuances that I struggled to decipher. Their sweat and their sacrifice would earn them the needed credibility with their funders. Their rootedness in their communities and their sensitivity to the issues in their country would best ensure they were not overlooked by relevant government programs. I was just fortunate to have been along for the ride.

As a result of that experience in Barbados, I have gained renewed perspective on the phrase "It's not what you know, it's who you know." In development, as in life, who you take on is almost as important as what you take on together. I now possess an eagerness to encounter wise souls wherever I journey and a hope that in whatever projects I undertake, I will find open-hearted collaborators.

5

In a Just World, Displacement Would Be Shocking

Alisha Nicole Apale

When I was twenty-three and nearly finished my under-graduate degree, my appetite for social change was grow-ing by leaps and bounds. It fed insatiably off a relatively new-found awareness of global social ills and their impact on health and disease around the world. At twenty-one, I didn't know who Nelson Mandela was. I had to look up terms like *colonialism* in the dictionary. My quest for infor-mation—for understanding—became almost frantic. I read, and read, and read some more. Often, I read too quickly, skipping the details as I looked for larger answers.

Throughout my last semester, I was consumed with choosing the perfect opportunity to launch my career: to get out there and respond to my earnest concern for the "poor and diseased." I discussed a few options with a close friend's father, explaining to him (as if he didn't already know) that too many people die unnecessarily. I reasoned that political will was the missing ingredient in social change. I thought I needed to get into politics to remedy the situation. He suggested I learn to work with the people around me, wherever life took me—that this would be more effective.

When I first set out to gain some work experience, I wanted to better understand the world of those who knew poverty, disease, war, and displacement first hand, those who embodied underdevelopment. I wanted to know if the situations described in documentaries, on the news, and in my novels and textbooks were really so intractable. Most of all, I couldn't bring myself to believe that so much injustice could persist if we all knew more about it. But as time went on, the idea of challenging "the system" and achieving social change became more and more daunting.

I went to the Thai–Burma border in October 2003.

In my suitcase I packed a belief dear to my heart: that the key to a more just world lies in creating greater awareness among the haves about the lives of the have-nots. I had painted the world with two broad strokes and believed that the "developed" world, which I saw as a place of power, was in need of mass education concerning the effects of our interactions, past and present, with the rest of the world. Perhaps if we were more aware of the externalities—the hidden costs—of our lifestyles, we would find it within ourselves to change. I had a hard time believing that the ills of the world exist because we allow them. I did not want to believe that persistent inequities were sometimes even intentional. I preferred to believe in innocence, or at least unintended error.

I left Montreal full of hope in the possibility of social change. My flight from Montreal to Bangkok aptly turned the world on its head for me. Mae Sot, the Thai border town known as "mini-Burma" where I was to end my journey, set aflame in me a far more nuanced perception of the world, humanity, and all our problems. Working with a community of non-status refugees along the Thai–Burma border was a most unforgiving dose of reality. For months following my glimpse into Burma, I was left shifting aimlessly on broken ground. It brought an abrupt end to the notion of social change as a thread in my career plan and entrenched it as a lifestyle—a deeply personal battle, fought from within and without.

SKIMMING ACROSS THAILAND

It is mid-morning in Bangkok when we touch down on the runway extravagantly framed by Thailand's finest greenery. Apprehensive and fatigued, I spend more than an hour staring at the sliding glass doors of the airport terminal exit. In my mind, the "developing world" lies behind those doors. After a now embarrassingly extended effort in personal coaching, I breathe through to my toes and move beyond what I believe is the last boundary.

"I want to go to the north bus station. How far is that? How many *baht*? Can you take me there?"

Thirty minutes later, I arrive at the north bus station. I hand a crisp five-hundred *baht* note to the driver as he places my bags on the sidewalk. Squaring my shoulders and heaving on my backpacks—one to the back, one to the front—and with IBM notebook in hand, I lift my eyes to the fast-paced atmosphere of the bus station. I am ready.

A young woman donned in Thai military apparel approaches. She nods. Her smile is firm, her eyes tender.

"Where are you going?" she inquires.

I quickly find myself in her care. She has convinced me that taking the night bus to Mae Sot is a terrible idea. Tourists do not go to Mae Sot. I insist that I am meeting friends there. "We plan to travel onward to Chiang Mai and other tourist areas ... ," as went the story suggested by the organization I was working through. It is true that tourists rarely go to Mae Sot. It contains one of Thailand's most persistent and contentious challenges: thousands of non-status refugees from Burma. With the bus due to arrive at 4:00 a.m., I am suddenly not so convinced about heading directly to the border town. Instead, I find myself on a bus crowded with Thai military personnel en route to Tak City, which lies about two hours east of Mae Sot. Although I had felt rather comfortable in the company of the young officer, only days afterward the experience of confronting anyone in military or police attire would send waves of fear through my limbs. A symbol of order and protection to many white middle-class Canadians like me, in Mae Sot, the police were a reminder of insecurity. They embodied the risk of imprisonment, hefty bribes, and even deportation. They were feared and avoided.

PLUNGING INTO BURMA

Mae Sot city is like a pool at the end of a steady stream of non-status refugees. On its outskirts sits Mae Pa village, a slightly more rural and remote setting. There I will spend the next months living among a well-established though discreet community of non-status refugees. About four days after my arrival in Thailand, with my orientation in Mae Sot complete, I move out to Mae Pa village. Arriving late in the afternoon, I meet the woman who has welcomed me to live with her and her extended family of twelve in the stilted two-room wooden house they rent.

The house neighbours the boarding school where I will teach and is a short walk to the offices of a student and youth congress—a political organization focused on democracy, national solidarity, and human rights—at which I will also soon work. As the sun sets, I head over to the school for dinner, as prearranged by my sending organization. A mountain of white rice is heaped onto a plate, flanked by bananas and a packet of Nescafé instant coffee, and placed in front of me. Not a moment later, a bowl of boiled vegetables is set down, teetering on the uneven planks of the wooden table. I eat slowly and watch as the children gather in front of a television, sprawling over each other, linking legs and arms or holding hands. They twirl playful fingers through one another's cropped black hair, styled to suit Thai fashion and create an illusion of belonging. I sit behind them, curious about their past, concerned for their future. After thanking them for my dinner, I cross the star-lit street toward my new home, although I hardly think of this place as anything resembling home. I do not belong here and that is as obvious to me as it is to them.

Why am I here?

That is the question that stirs me throughout the night, despite concerted efforts to quiet my mind into some semblance of rest.

As soon as night is broken by the first soft beams of the sun, the house is abuzz. Foremost on my agenda for the day is the class of students waiting for me to teach them English. I close my eyes, checking my anxieties. It is not a good day when the first thing on your to-do list seems so far out of reach. I feel completely unprepared. Regardless, I gear up and convince myself that after breakfast I will feel better. I can do this.

As I eat, "K," the director of the orphanage, hands me a publication entitled *License to Rape*.[1] He's heard that I'm interested in women's health issues, and although I'm still shedding my sleepiness, he proceeds to elaborate on the narratives documented in the report. He details women's experiences of rape, sexual assault, and slavery: atrocities that are far more approachable when distanced by academia, when sterilized by statistics. My body tingles, alerted to the realities of life on the border.

K, who shaped much of my experience on the border and dominates most of my memories of Burma, still speaks to me unceasingly. Having survived ten years as a political prisoner, K, a teacher by profession, is driven by one memory: On witnessing his students fall to their deaths in the 1988 student-led protests against Burma's dictators, he will never forget that no one came to help. Still hearing their shouts of protest and their cries for democracy, he embarked on a flight from Burma that was day by day encumbered by an ever-increasing collection of orphaned and abandoned children. Conversations with K are consistently preceded and concluded by the narrative of their plight, one that presents an agonizing challenge to anyone who believes in the concept of justice, to anyone who calls human life beautiful. His experiences, of which I caught only a glimpse, are such that he addresses a mother seeking help for her raped toddler with a kind of professionalism; he offers quiet empathy, support, and protection. He shows little distress because he is not surprised. I, on the other hand, fold away into a corner. Useless. Crying at the sight of that fragile little girl.

Unfortunately, K has been unfairly labelled by many of the border's expatriate workers as a frustratingly embittered, chronically depressed, and highly difficult man to work with. He also concretely illustrates the indignities of sustained dependence on donor handouts. When resources are donated to the orphanage, always on an emergency basis and never through a comprehensive strategy of poverty alleviation, they are quickly consumed. And just as surely, they are depleted. Once again, K is left working with only the shoddy remainders of an inadequate donation meant to support this community of seventy-five orphaned and abandoned children. The story of dwindling resources, coupled with a heightening chorus of reminders, are rehearsed at the beginning and conclusion of every single one of our encounters. At a rate of about three or four meetings per day, K's reminders are well entrenched in my mind: "Alisha, they treat us like animals. We lived in the jungle like animals. But, if I have to be an animal, I will not be a lamb. I will be a lion."

His analogy of animal-like treatment refers primarily to the actions of the Burmese military government, the source of suffering for the Burmese people. It refers to the way he, and many others like him, were hunted down as they raced to cross the border. But he is also referring to the Thai government's policies on Burmese refugees and, frequently, to the more elusive "international community." K and his students are living the experience of being a neglected issue, a disposable people. They are an ad hoc assembly of displaced persons with no legal status. In spite of obvious need, there are far too many bureaucratic hoops to jump through to gain the reliable support of most NGOs in the region, or elsewhere.

Day after day, when I push open the heavy wooden shutters, the rural Thai landscape—with its rolling hills and lush rice paddies—floods into the small room I share with two young girls. I am transported back to the *National Geographic* magazines that my father used to read, the very ones I used to tease him about as a teenager. To me, he read of an imaginary world. To many friends back home, chronically infected with the travel bug, my position here would be envious. But at the time, I certainly would not have described my journey as anything enviable. My world—my ideas, aspirations, expectations—was quickly unravelling.

In the world beyond the border, the word *Burma* often conjures up an underwhelming response. The Burma issue waxes and wanes in the geopolitical and public consciousness, a rhythm that seems to be set by the coverage, or lack thereof, of "breaking news" stories. According to its prime minister in exile, Sein Win, the problem with Burma is that "its crisis is too old; it cannot capitalize on the novelties and freshness of situations like Darfur."[2]

A few months after I left the border, I joined the Burma Solidarity Collective (BSC) at McGill University. In an effort to share some information about the country, I worked with the collective to enhance and publicize the BSC website. Having sent the link to some contacts, I was left trying to understand the lack of reaction from the majority of recipients. I rationalized it as a question of timing. Christmas holidays were encroaching, people were busy. I found that typical but unsettling. At the same time, I also recognized that it *was* unfair of me to question apathy. After all, before I had left for Thailand, I didn't "care" about the people of Burma. I didn't know about them. Perhaps most unsettling of all was that my theory—that if we knew more, we'd do more—was being disproved.

DECEMBER 31, 2004

I sit in a church, tears angrily forcing themselves beyond my eyelids.

It is five days after the 2004 Southeast Asian tsunami and nine months since I left the border. As the numbers pour in, each vanishing soul matters less. It has to. For some, resilience demands it; for others, growing numbers produce a greater degree of disconnection. It is true. The death of one is a tragedy. The death of many only reinforces the norm of life on the margins.

In an effort to comfort me, someone said, "It is sad, Alisha, I know. But they are used to dying over there."

Following the tsunami, donations flooded in to support international rescue operations. It consumed the largest financial donation I personally doled out that year. I remember sitting at my computer, clicking a box here, filling in a credit card number there. I felt good about it. For a time. For the next year I received thank-you emails documenting the effects of donations like mine, telling me how a second donation could help even more.

On further reflection, I was increasingly distressed at how this manner of responding to the world's troubles can so easily satisfy one's conscience. As much as was possible, while working on the border, I had connected with a group of people who lived life on the periphery. The community I lived in was no longer a faceless populace, no longer a matter of statistics or a group of people who matter insomuch as they illustrate the ills of the world. Or at least they should not have been. Yet there I was, satisfying my contribution to social change—the astonishingly rapid and generous mobilization of aid in the face of crisis—with a credit card.

DISCONNECTEDNESS

Shared suffering does not always result in unity.

While on the border, time spent with the expatriate community was deemed cathartic. But evenings spent at a local bar, cold beer in hand, threw me a curveball. It was akin to a model United Nations event run amok. Young experts-in-training carelessly throwing hefty opinions around, as if the issues were devoid of genuine human suffering. Conversations were fuelled by a steady undercurrent of largely unconstructive criticism. Many organizations on the border were structured on shared ethnic identity, not necessarily shared cause. They were connected by a common circumstance, namely the experience of living as refugees without official status on the Thai–Burma border. And they worked toward their various causes under a common rubric: achieving democracy in Burma. Still, intercommunity rivalries were common, and these frictions were quickly adopted by expatriates and used as evidence that civil war would soon follow the collapse of Burma's military government, if it was ever achieved.

One of the organizations I worked with was particularly criticized, and I found myself in the unsolicited position of representing an ethnic community labelled as a near-supremacist, nationalistic group of separatists. Having worked with more than one ethnic community and also with a *multi*-ethnic organization, I knew that to some extent each community harboured a degree of nationalistic sentiment. Yet such sentiments were hardly tolerated by most of the expatriates. "The people of Burma must stick together," they proclaimed.

But why? Burma has not always been a sovereign nation. Formerly part of India, Burma is yet another imaginary state, a lumping together of diverse ethnic and religious communities in a manner suitable for colonial exploits. As young development workers fresh on the scene, who are we to decide what constitutes unity? Who are we to dictate that the best way forward for Burma is through the development of a single democratic state?

Just as shared suffering does not necessarily beget unity, not everyone experiences dissent in the same way. The experience of being a "refugee," with or without status, is wildly diverse and I often found myself trying to balance one experience or opinion against the next. For some, the experience of seeking refuge was made possible by having the means to get out. I recall joyriding in northern Thailand in Saya's Mercedes Benz. A high-powered Buddhist abbot from Burma, Saya was regularly consulted by other high-powered men from Burma at his palatial monastery. Cruising the Salween River one afternoon in a motorboat, he took me to see an SPDC camp on the Burmese side of the river.[3]

"Do you see that flag over there?" he asked

"Yes. Whose is it?"

"That is a military camp."

"Sorry?" The engine and wind made it difficult to hear him. He didn't just say "military camp," did he?

"It is a military camp. The SPDC operate from there." My eyes betray deep concern. "Do not worry. We're fine out here. You are safe with me!"

The majority of people I met on the border, however, did not have quite so comfortable an experience of seeking refuge as did this man. For many, seeking refuge was an acute action taken to avoid (further) imprisonment or death and involved leaving loved ones behind. "I left my mother, father, and fiancée. I don't know where my siblings are. I had to leave. My family was threatened because of my political views. I want democracy. So do they. But my parents are old now and it is up to my generation. I did not tell my fiancée anything. I just left one night. I could not risk her life too. She doesn't know where I am or why I left."

As they sorted their way through the process of gaining status from the United Nations High Commissioner for Refugees, most of the people I got to know on the border described the decision to seek status as a controversial one. For some, seeking status involved depoliticizing themselves, their experiences, and their vision for Burma. It was a matter of prioritizing basic needs over the collective political struggle, a means of garnering some level of security, a way of moving forward. It allowed life to be lived, albeit in an unjust world. On the border, this was sometimes seen as selling out, capitulating to a world order that demands being part of a nation-state *prior* to a cause or belief. Other people I knew refused the label *refugee* altogether.

"I am *not* a refugee. I am a person demanding my right for freedom. I will never be a refugee."

Others, undecided about how to proceed, struggled with the implications of accepting refugee status, a label believed to take away autonomy and one's purpose in life.

"If I take refugee status, then what can I do? I will be forced to stay in a camp and wait—maybe for the rest of my life—for something to change. At least here I have a few freedoms. I have some dignity."

For others, seeking status was strategic, an alternative way to further the democratic cause. It was a way of getting out into the "free world" to foster greater awareness about Burma.

"I can only work toward the freedom of my people if I am free to do so. I have to leave this place at the first opportunity."

The border is a place where ten-year-olds are fluent in human rights, democracy, and social justice discourse. To me, a child's fluency on these issues speaks most clearly to their absence. It also seems to support Romeo Dallaire's conclusion on the Rwandan genocide—that some people matter and some people do not. When one is awash in insecurity, protecting oneself, one's family, and one's community from further adversity demands a life of caution. It was only after four months of living there and one bittersweet conversation with Soe, a colleague and friend, that I began to understand this.

We sat on an expansive balcony, welcoming the cool night air as it absorbed the heat and fatigue of the day. Lazy conversation about the day's events drifted into the story of Soe's journey from his home in west Burma to Mae Pa village. Unveiling layers of his experience, he chronicled a sequence of events fit for the big screen.

His story left me speechless. After a long silence, I noted that we had shared many conversations and asked what made him decide to tell me this today.

He laughed easily, as he always did. Then, after a lengthy pause, he replied in an uncharacteristically flat tone, "Alisha, identities can easily be forged."

Confused, I shake my head. "I don't understand."

He went on to explain that it was not until then that he thought it sufficiently proven that I was not a spy working on behalf of the Burmese military, the Thai security police, or the CIA.

STOP. START

It is midweek and the sun is already setting. I have finished teaching my class at a nearby political organization later than usual. Rushing back to the school and up a steep stairway to the upper room, I see K's figure shadowing the doorway. He tells me to eat quickly.

"We must talk. We need to discuss our situation."

My mind races through the near-endless scenarios. Are we running short on rice again? Was one of the students arrested and deported? Did my recent late-night conversation about love and sex with some of the girls at the school breach the line of "appropriate matters to discuss with your students"?

Dinner, albeit cold, sated my hunger. I cross the floor, gingerly tiptoeing through a maze of children, some sleeping, some studying, some watching television, and join K on the balcony. The air is cool and the sky is star strewn.

"Alisha, we must close the school for another week. The monks have told us that the Thai government is tired of our presence."

The news is frustrating. The stop–start nature of our programs impedes our progress. While it is not good news, we are grateful for the friendship of the Mae Pa abbot, who is well connected with local Thai authorities and often leaks information to protect K and the students.

"Alisha, like the world, the Thai government cares only for economics, for money. Refugees are neither good for the economy nor suitable for international business interests."

I refrain from pointing out what he already knows. Hundreds of status and non-status refugees line the conveyor belts of Mae Sot's factories. Working on the front lines of the garment industry, they are crucial links in a global supply chain that is a huge asset to international business interests. Yet Thailand's king would soon celebrate his birthday and for the occasion he wishes to portray a country well suited to tourism and international business. Burmese refugees, who do not figure well into the national image he wishes to portray, ought to hunker down lest they be detained, deported, or otherwise removed during the national clean-up.

As has become the norm, our discussion lapses into the realm of human rights and social justice. "We need to persist when seeking justice, peace, and freedom," K recites. "Even the international community does not recognize us as humans. They do not support our fight. They turn us away while we suffer like animals."

Closing the school once again means that the children's studies will be interrupted. With exams approaching, the biggest hindrance to success is not ability, confidence, or determination. Rather, alongside the challenges of limited funding, food, and supplies, the stop–start of the children's classes due to security concerns represents an enormous barrier. According to many community members, the biggest threat to the SPDC is education. This is the issue over which K and the SPDC concur. Knowledge and awareness are what the SPDC fears most. Education has become an all-important currency in the global division between the haves and have-nots. It is also what schools and organizations like the ones I taught in are willing to risk everything for.

When describing the power struggle between the SPDC and people like himself, K pinpoints the ultimate driver in the SPDC's oppression: "They fear an open mind. They know that education brings awareness, and awareness brings protest. It is the students they fear. They fear those who learn of, work and live for, justice. We may not be armed, but we are a kind of freedom fighter."

As a form of protest, we decide to continue our classes, albeit behind tightly closed doors. I am aware of the risks I take personally. They are relatively few. Much more predominant in my mind is the risk taken by the students I teach. During this particular security threat— and there were many—two students are arrested in the market and deported. Being able to pay the charges levied by local traffickers, they are back in Mae Pa within a week, though once again broke and shaken.

Although K constantly asks if I have told others about the situation—"Tell all your Canadian friends. Tell them about us so that they will know our real situation"—I seldom write home during this period. It is not for a lack of things to write, but for lack of clarity on *how* to write.

"K, I do write to my friends in Canada, but I worry about how they will read it. I worry that if I don't use the right words, I will be sensationalizing these things, that it will not be accurate."

Offended, K tells me sternly that his life is not fiction. "This is not a story. This is our real situation. This is our life. If they do not believe it, tell them to come. I welcome them. I want them to know, to be aware and to join in our protest. With or without them, I will fight this freedom fight until my very last breath."

Almost without motion, he gets up. I remain seated. Sitting cross-legged on the cool wooden floor, silent under a starry sky, I am left to ponder all that's been said, and everything that has gone unsaid.

IF ILLUSION IS WHAT WE WANT

The only thing more ad hoc about daily life on the border is the kind and quality of information the students have access to. In this, and so many other ways, their experiences stand in sharp contrast to those whose lives are almost cluttered by inordinate access to information and opportunity. Yet as I was beginning to learn, awareness and the opportunity to act on it do not *necessarily* change anything. Back in the Mae Pa school house, a collection of outdated, threadbare textbooks and a subscription to a national newspaper were the primary connections the students had to the outside world. As an educated foreigner responsible for setting my own curriculum, I could have stood in front of my classes and said just about anything. Of all the things I did say, I highly regret that the one piece of information I failed to deliver could quite possibly have been the most truthful. It might also have been the most derailing.

I should have told them that ceaseless efforts to broadcast their plight to the world fall by and large on deaf ears. Few people seem to know about Burma—or the experiences of those living along the border. Among those who do know, few have any substantial ideas on how to achieve real change. Education, as K stated, may bring awareness. But it doesn't necessarily mobilize the kind of action needed to achieve fundamental and lasting change; it doesn't necessarily bring justice. It was a lesson I had not yet learned for myself.

Years later, as I look out of the dust-speckled windows of my apartment in Nairobi, I still struggle to form a coherent response to the realities I encountered on the Border. I still regularly receive emails from my Burmese friends and colleagues. Many of them are informational, passing along the latest reports of grassroots efforts working tirelessly toward democracy and human rights. Others are more personal, reminiscing about our time spent together in the border town we all temporarily called home. Still others reflect on what may be a common experience for those who have worked in a similar context. They reflect what is probably a universal human experience: of having expectations and then facing disappointment. They entail questions such as "Why don't you write more often?"; "Why don't you send money?"; and "Why—like everyone else—do you seem to have forgotten us?" One particularly stinging email left me reeling. "Teacher, you lie," it began. My former student goes on to tell me that he hates me and that I am no better than anyone else. Emphatic, he notes that I too have dismissed their plight.

The people of Burma have been fighting for human rights and democracy for decades. Appeals for recognition and support have never ceased. I left the Thai–Burma border more conflicted than I cared to admit. Raw. Almost jaded. To date, my response to the questions "Why don't you care?" and "How do you cope?" remains incomplete. I wanted to move beyond the shock of my experiences. In a just world, displacement would be shocking. But we don't live in a just world, and displacement is everyday life for millions.

After my time on the border came to an end, my return to Montreal was met by a prolonged period of silence. I met many new people, none of whom had engaged in any form of development work. Perhaps ironically, many of these new friends had, however, grown up in developing countries. I was quickly fatigued with the hint of fascination in their questions about my decision to go to the Thai–Burma border: my decision to put myself purposely in "such a place," to choose to experience "those conditions." I was also viscerally resistant to the presumption of goodness attributed to development workers. For months after returning from the border, the corridors of my mind echoed with forms of silence, some of anger, some of disappointment, some, even, of dismissal. All were necessary for me as I began to weave life on the border into my experience of daily life back at "home."

For most of my life, I have lived among people who have the opportunity to matter. Learning to live among people who do not has forced me to stare humanity in the face. Lessons on this aspect of being human have not been limited to the Thai–Burma border. These lessons follow me as I move across other countries and continents, taunting and provoking me. On a night train heading west from Delhi, my sleep is pierced by the screams of a homeless child being whipped for stowing a ride. I am shaken, but I prefer to stay in the safe confines of my bunk than to confront the horrid scene. Walking in downtown Montreal, I turn a street corner to face a homeless man being beaten. With each kick to his gut, I recoil further, wishing I were blind. Seated in a late-night bus in Nairobi, I feel the window panes clapped in a cacophony of sweaty palms as street boys beg for money. They motion with their open mouths, as if to fill my ears with the echoes of their hollow bellies. I wish I were deaf.

Maybe the kid on that Delhi train should not have stowed a ride, I rationalize. The rules are clear. If you want to take the train, you have to buy a ticket. Besides, I am in a foreign country. I do not speak their language. It would be foolish to get involved.

It probably would not have been smart—or safe—for me to try to break up that Montreal street scene. After all, they were just roughing him up a bit. He will be fine. He will be just fine.

I should not have been in downtown Nairobi that late in the evening anyway. I could get mugged if I get off this bus. Even if I give those kids a few shillings, tomorrow they will be hungry again. Besides, I barely have enough cash on hand for my fare home. What if there is an emergency?

I shudder at how disconnected we are from one another. And then, I move on.

My responses to Burma—and to the development industry and its relation to social change—have involved a process of extracting expectations from reality. It has been an exercise in accepting disappointment as a natural human experience. It has involved coming face to face with the flaws of being human.

No longer shocked by displacement, I am instead shocked at how limited is our capacity to care for others. I am disturbed at how infrequently education and awareness result in action or change. I am concerned about how easily daily life in Canada slips by. Time moves on, few things really change, and injustice—this interminable characteristic of being human—weaves its way through life, endlessly assaulting its favourite victims.

In some ways, the media hype surrounding the 2004 Southeast Asian tsunami, or any other tragedy on any other given day, is akin to drawing a highlighter across a plethora of social ills: events that are noted and chronicled. But for what purpose? What do we do with this information? At that New Year's Eve service, why did we take time to remember lost souls? Why did we call for blessings on those who live lives we call miserable, on those who live displacement day in and day out? Why do we congratulate ourselves on cash flow sparked by tragedy? Knowing that the evening marks a tradition of resolutions and fresh beginnings, I cried. I felt shame.

Were I to return to the border area—and had the Thai government's most recent clean sweep not further displaced many of the people I lived and worked with—would I be brave enough, after so much silence, to seek K out? The children at the orphanage? The family I lived with? My colleagues? If I met with them, would I tell them all I told Soe? Would it be fair to tell them that few people know or actively care about the problems of Burma? Would it be appropriate to advise them to stop hoping, as they so often did, for an Iraq-style invasion by the United States to come and overthrow the SPDC? Would it be too defeatist to dispel their wish for a miracle NGO to come and fund the orphanage for the rest of time? Would it be self-righteous to advise them against promoting one ethnic community of Burma over another, to work together at all costs?

And then, I ask myself, what would give me the right to take away hope from people who've already been robbed of so much?

From time to time, I still ponder the advice given by my friend's father. Perhaps unfortunately, I have come to view policy and law as more crucial to social change than aid or charity. When discussing these issues with friends or colleagues, I sometimes suggest that perhaps social justice ought to be legislated if it is to be achieved. My suggestion betrays the painful experience of losing my faith in humanity. But it has helped me to distinguish social change from the development industry and its overwhelmingly emotional appeal. And while I have largely moved beyond my disappointment with how infrequently awareness changes anything, I seem unable to accept that another way forward isn't possible.

6

Salama, vazaha!
Maro Adjemian

A trans-Atlantic flight from Montreal to Paris, a long stop-over, and another, longer flight to the capital of Madagascar, Antananarivo, are already behind me. I am finally on a small plane from Antananarivo en route to Fort Dauphin, the town where I will spend the next six months. I strain to keep my eyes open, struggling against fatigue, and try to soak up the countryside far below my window. Red earth, sprinkled with occasional small patches of forest. Madagascar. I am really here.

The plane curves around the deep blue of the Indian Ocean bay and touches down on the runway with a bump. I swallow to clear my ears, swing my backpack onto my shoulder, and hang my wool sweater over my arm: a remnant from a colder climate now far away. I stumble out, exhausted, into the hot air. Smiling staff from Azafady, the NGO I will be working with for the next six months, have come to pick me up. I am packed into an old Peugeot taxi that swerves along potholed roads to the house that serves as the Azafady office.

Driving through town, we pass colours that are rich and strong: the red earth, turquoise sea, lush green vegetation, brilliant flowers and birds. Even the people wear richly coloured clothing. The women wrap their all-purpose *lamba hoany*, rectangular cloths covered in vibrant patterns, around their waists to protect their clothes as they work. They also use their *lamba hoany* to tie their babies to their backs, the little head emerging at the top to nod contentedly against his mother's back as she goes about her daily routine.

When we arrive at the office, I am introduced to the Azafady staff, both Malagasy and foreign. I am welcomed into the little back room behind the office that will be my home for the next six months. In the evening, they offer me rice and fresh vegetables and brochettes of *zebu*, the Malagasy humped cow, with hot sauce.

Finally, when night has fallen, I lie on my new bed in my new room, cozily listening to the rain pounding on the roof. Exhausted yet exhilarated, I feel the day's sights and sounds and smells wash over me. Crashing turquoise waves at the edge of the town; tiny shacks with dirt floors; barefoot, shyly smiling children; men walking down the road with live pigs slung over their shoulders; species of trees I have never seen even in photos ... and the sleep I have been pushing off for so many hours finally envelops me.

BEGINNINGS

Fort Dauphin, where Azafady is based, is the largest town in southeastern Madagascar. It is on a peninsula lined with white sandy beaches, jutting out into the Indian Ocean. The town is a sprawl of dirt roads and sandy paths connecting small wooden, cement, and palm-branch houses, tiny shops, a few small restaurants and bars, and a huge market. There are often a handful of tourists in Fort Dauphin, who come mostly to enjoy the beaches and nearby national parks. There are also a few other NGOs in town, bringing in foreigners from various parts of the world. However, white faces are few and far between enough that *vazaha*, as foreigners are called, are novel and exciting. Everywhere I walk I hear constant calls of "Salama, vazaha" (Hello, foreigner).

Azafady focuses on conservation and sustainable development in Fort Dauphin and the surrounding area. It aims to increase people's standard of living while conserving the local natural resources. During my internship I will be working for their Sustainable Livelihoods initiative. The goal is to provide sustainable methods of improving food security and nutrition in rural areas, as well as to introduce small, sustainable income-generating projects.

Before I left for Madagascar, I knew I wanted to work in the field of sustainable international development but felt disillusioned with development projects I had studied. I questioned whether willing people such as I from the wealthy West could be of any real use to people living in developing countries. How could I teach agriculture to people who had lived as subsistence farmers for generations? How could I encourage people to plant trees rather than cutting them when I knew they needed wood to build their houses and cook their meals, and when I used more paper in a week than they did in a year? What, practically, could I ever do that would be of any use to developing countries?

Reading the description of the Sustainable Livelihoods project on the Azafady website, I had thought it looked like a perfect example of a small, grassroots organization striving to carry out sustainable, practical projects in partnership with the local community. Well aware that websites can be deceiving, I told myself that no matter what, my six-month internship would be an incredible learning experience. Either I would learn how such projects could be carried out successfully or I would learn pitfalls to avoid. Or perhaps a bit of both.

I meet with Brett, the director and founder of Azafady, a couple of days after I first arrive in Madagascar. He tells me more about the organization and instructs me to let him know when I have a clearer idea of what I would like to do during my internship. Azafady has no experience with interns like me who arrive, fully funded, for six months with no defined project of their own. All the other foreign

volunteers have raised money to carry out a specific project. I appreciate the freedom Brett gives me, but having just arrived I have no clear
idea of where I can fit in or how I can be the most useful.

Through conversations with Malagasy members of the Azafady
staff, I gradually come up with the idea of researching and developing
small-scale aquaculture. I find out that people in "the bush," as anywhere outside the town of Fort Dauphin is called, are interested in
such a project but that no one has begun working on it yet. As a biolo-
gist, I am, in general, sceptical about the benefits of aquaculture. I have
heard too many examples of environmental problems being caused
by such projects: the destructive waste of marine species used as fish
food, accidental introductions of foreign invasive species, the spread of
disease. The aquaculture projects I will be researching in Madagascar,
however, are of a completely different scale. They are small-scale fish
farms where fish are enclosed in a pond and kept available as a source
of food and income.

Members of the Azafady staff tell me that small-scale farming of
herbivore fish could be a valuable addition to the Sustainable Livelihoods initiative, both as a source of protein and as a small income-
generating project for the village communities. People eat fish when
it is available, and some people regularly walk up to twenty-five kilometres to the coast to buy fish and trade them in their villages. However, in most of the villages where Azafady works the population lives
almost entirely on starches, and malnutrition is widespread.

A local Malagasy NGO has already begun freshwater aquaculture
projects in several villages in the area. This allows me to visit these projects and ask questions, along with my faithful guide and interpreter,
Roly. Our research involves long trips for several days at a time to small
villages in the bush. We stay with families who own fishponds in these
villages, helping them with the work involved to maintain them in
exchange for information and an occasional meal of fresh fish. I also
contact people in Fort Dauphin who have experience in aquaculture
for any help they might be able to give. The projects we visit and learn
about are simple enough: easily maintained small ponds dug in the

path of a water source. They provide a home for herbivore fish that can be fed rice husks and other vegetable waste. There are many local species of fish that would be appropriate for such a project. The landscape in the bush where Azafady works is perfect for constructing such ponds: criss-crossing streams and rivers, hills to ensure constant water flow, and clay soil that is good at retaining water.

IMMERSION

As my internship develops, my time is divided between working on the aquaculture project with Roly, and working with Latena, the Sustainable Livelihoods co-ordinator, to monitor and expand the existing projects. My work with Latena shows me how effective a partnership can be between local, dedicated people and *vazaha* who bring a broader perspective.

Ten days after I arrive in Fort Dauphin, I am sent on a trip to the bush with Latena to check up on the existing projects. Our visit to the bush will require taking a *taxi-brousse* (Malagasy public transportation) until the road ends, and then hiking the rest of the way on tiny paths. When I tell the other foreign staff at Azafady about the plan for our trip, they are surprised.

"Just you and Latena, no one else?"

"He's so serious."

"He's very quiet. After three months here, I still don't know him very well."

But I like Latena from the start. He is a tall, thin man in his forties who has eight children ranging in age from eight to twenty. He was originally hired as Azafady's artist, to illustrate booklets developed to explain their projects. Since most people in the bush are illiterate, clear illustrations are a necessary component of educational material. Three months before I came to Madagascar the *vazaha* founder of the Sustainable Livelihoods initiative left, leaving Latena in charge. By the time I arrive, he is juggling his artist tasks with his position as co-ordinator. Working closely with Latena throughout my internship teaches me far more about sustainable development than any course or book ever could. My respect for him grows as I watch him work, and I get to know him not only as a colleague, interpreter, and language teacher but also as a friend.

Our first trip to the bush is my initiation into *taxi-brousse* travel. We wait for our ride at the Fort Dauphin *taxi-brousse* station, a chaotic open area in the middle of the market. Vehicles of various shapes and sizes and states of disrepair are parked on the sandy ground. Occasionally they arrive or leave, honking their horns and manoeuvring their way through the commotion. Drivers call out their destinations to recruit passengers. Market vendors wind their way through the crowds with baskets or trays of wares.

There are transport truck *taxi-brousses*, pickup truck *taxi-brousses*, and ancient station wagon *taxi-brousses*. All of them have the ability to drive on terrible roads, although most break down on a regular basis. And they all have in common the ability to transport more people at once than you would think physically possible, along with all their miscellaneous baggage.

Taxi-brousses also share the unpredictability of their departure times, although after one is used to their comings and goings, the pattern of unpredictability results in its own version of predictability. After regular *taxi-brousse* travel, for example, I notice that they generally leave the station approximately two hours late. Once I realize this, every time I hear a departure time quoted, I simply add two hours in my head and am usually fairly close to the actual time. Of course, this rule does not always hold true. Once I was meant to leave at 6:00 p.m. and did not actually leave until 3:30 p.m. the following day! And I know that if I arrive at the station two hours late, there is always the chance that, for once, it has quickly filled up, left close to on time, and I have missed my ride. I learn to take the attitude of the Malagasy to avoid frustration: I am fortunate to have a ride at all. Does it really matter if I leave earlier or later, as long as I eventually arrive at my destination?

It takes three hours to jolt and bounce the thirty-five kilometres to a town called Mahatalaky, through puddles large enough to be called small lakes and huge, rocky holes, often off the road altogether and through fields in order to avoid the worst patches. Mahatalaky marks the end of the road; from there on we will walk along small paths to the dispersed villages where Azafady works. We stop for lunch in Mahatalaky at a tiny restaurant where only one meal-of-the-day is offered: a heaping bowl of rice and meat or fish to go with it, for the equivalent of about a dollar Canadian. Damy and Maka, the extension workers, meet us at the restaurant to accompany us to the villages we will visit.

It is Latena's idea to have extension workers continually carrying out work in the bush, allowing the projects to develop from within the communities themselves. Damy and Maka are two motivated men from different villages who are willing to try out Sustainable Livelihoods projects as examples and to teach people in their own and surrounding villages the techniques for a small salary. Latena is also determined to spread Sustainable Livelihoods projects to the remote, inland villages and focus less on the coastal villages, which already have many resources brought to them from the sea. When I arrive in Madagascar, projects exist in four villages: two coastal and two inland.

We follow the trails that wind through the countryside: flat fields, rolling hills, grassland with a few scattered bushes and trees. Frequently, streams and rivers cut through our path and we cross over them on a single log that has been placed across the water as a bridge. Where there is no log, we wade through the water to the other side.

Every once in a while we pass a small area of lush, untouched rain forest standing lonely in a landscape of grassland and low bushes. Latena explains to me that these areas are cemeteries. Ancestors and the dead are very revered in Malagasy culture. It is forbidden to cut or take any vegetation from an area where people have been buried. So these tiny islands of forest have been conserved, providing a mocking glimpse of what much of the entire island must have once looked like in stark contrast to our present surroundings. At one time, huge areas of Madagascar were covered with forest, teeming with plants and animals found nowhere else on earth. And now, in a country that is approximately 85 per cent deforested, only small patches remain.

During this initial trip to the bush Latena and I visit only three villages to evaluate the status of the existing projects. Each village contains several hamlets; each hamlet is a grouping of tiny huts made of palm branches, thatched with palm leaves, and suspended above the ground by short wooden stilts at each corner. As we wind our way between the houses and hamlets we see men harvesting rice, women rhythmically pounding rice from its husks with wooden mortar and pestles, small boys herding *zebu*, girls seated on the ground weaving baskets from sisal fibres, and small children playing. Everyone we pass always stops whatever they are doing to stare at me, and some shyly call, "Salama, vazaha."

I spend most of the time trying to soak in and understand everything that is going on around me. I want to learn the local dialect of the Malagasy language as much as possible so that I will be able to understand and communicate without constant dependence on an interpreter. Latena is a good language teacher. Often, he speaks to me in Malagasy and makes me struggle to understand for a while before he will translate. He also sometimes leaves me by myself to 'practise my Malagasy' with the people in the bush who speak nothing else. This immersion into Malagasy bush daily life and language is tiring, but very exciting.

During the six months I work with him, Latena changes the system of developing community groups. Rather than assembling interested community members and designating a leader, he forms groups within the context of family clans. The villages where we work are very remote, and the traditional family clan is still an important institution. By naming a clan responsible for a project with the respected elder as the leader, Latena works within already existing systems, thus avoiding—or at least limiting—conflict.

Latena's priority is sustainability. More than once, he tells me that in order to be sustainable a project must be adopted into a given community and culture. It must be adapted and made their own. It must be simple enough to begin and maintain that people will take the idea, modify it to fit their needs, and show it to their family and neighbours in turn.

Throughout our time working together, Latena asks my advice on decisions. He always respects my views and takes the time to interpret for me and to discuss issues. Because of this I feel comfortable expressing my opinion, asking questions, and telling him my ideas. I am confident that his final decisions will be thoughtful and effective.

THE PIED PIPER

I learn that my name, Maro, is also a Malagasy word that means "many," or "a lot." In Madagascar, for the first time of my life, I hear my name spoken regularly. I am interested to discover that it appears on the map of Madagascar quite frequently: towns have names such as "many crocodiles," "many stones," or "many mosquitoes." When I introduce myself, the normal reaction is initial disbelief, and then the question, "Why do you have a Malagasy name?" I explain that my name has a different meaning where I come from, and the people I am speaking to usually nod thoughtfully, trying politely to hide their confusion.

Sometimes people accidentally call me "Mora." *Mora* is a Malagasy word that can mean slow, stupid, cheap, or easy, depending on the context. No matter which meaning I choose to attribute to it, I don't see how I can take the name as a compliment.

Several of the gardens in various villages have been neglected, due either to group conflicts or to other priorities in people's busy lives. In one village where we work, however, Latena and I are pleased to find a vegetable garden that is a work of art. A member of the village, Tsirava Paul, has mobilized a large group of people to diligently care for a huge and beautiful garden. There is not a weed in the beds, and every plant has been carefully watered and fertilized with manure. The villagers have a reason: they want to sell their vegetables in the market to raise money to build a school. Currently there is no school in the village, and only two people, one of them Tsirava Paul, have gone to elementary school.

In the village of the beautiful garden, Latena and I stay in the Azafady "pharmacy": the tiny palm-thatched hut built as a dispensary for malaria medication. During our first day, we meet with Tsirava Paul, the president of the village, and a few other important community members to discuss the status of the project. We sit in a circle on the floor of the pharmacy to carry out our meeting. As we talk, curious children begin to gather at the open doorway and window. Soon, both are completely filled with small faces.

When we have finished our meeting and the village members have left to go about their work, I decide to try to make friends with our curious onlookers. But as soon as I stand up and move toward the doorway, the children all scatter like frightened wild animals. I sit down outside the door and wait patiently. They slowly trickle back, a few at a time, until many of them are sitting around me. Some are even bold enough to brush up against me a tiny bit. One of them shyly offers me a piece of sugarcane, and they are all extremely amused at my efforts to rip pieces off with my teeth.

They also think it is hilarious when I try to talk to them with my limited Malagasy vocabulary. One question I know how to ask is "How old are you?" But every child I ask gives me the same answer: "I don't know." It is the same in many villages: they have no official identification documents, and no one has bothered to remember exactly when their children were born.

Later on, Latena suggests that it is time to wash our hands, faces, and feet as we have been busy hiking and transplanting tree seedlings all morning. He asks one of the children, a beautiful little girl, if she can show us where to go to wash. She eagerly leads the way along a path, down to the river. At one point during the walk I look behind me and cannot help laughing out loud. Winding along the path behind me in single file is a very long line of children, zigzagging up the hillside and finally disappearing into a grove of coffee trees. Maro the Pied Piper! They all gather around me at the river's edge and watch in fascination as I scrub my hands and feet.

The next evening we are once again squashed into the pharmacy, talking to Tsirava Paul and some other community members. A few children have sneaked in to observe the exciting events. The same little girl who showed us the river is sitting beside me. She tries to be as close to me as possible throughout our visit, although she is rarely brave enough to touch me. She just sits and looks at me, with huge, dark, admiring eyes.

During the afternoon, the president of the next village over had given Latena and me the special gift of half a litre of warm, flat Coca-Cola from the tiny shop in his house. We saved it until the evening to share with the community during our meeting, and now bring it out. Once the adults have had their share, I give the half-empty bottle to the little girl to distribute among the children. She carefully pours a tiny bit into the bottom of a cup and gives it to the boy beside her. He sips it slowly and reverently down to the last drop and hands the cup back to her. She pours another tiny bit into the cup and passes it to the next child. When everyone has had a taste, she gives the bottle, still with a bit of Coke in it, back to me. I tell her to finish it, and she repeats the same patient process of distribution as before. All the children are silent and polite, their eyes shining with excitement.

The little girl is sad to see us go when we leave the next morning, but I assure her that I will come back again soon. When we return a few weeks later she is not the only one eager to see me. As we approach the village, the children come running to meet us, calling, "Maro! Maro! Salama, Maro!" It is the first time people in the bush have ever called me by name rather than simply *vazaha*, and it makes me so happy I want to laugh out loud and gather them all up into my arms. They know my name!

BUSH TRAVEL

After my brief introductory trip to the bush, my visits with Latena become regular monthly excursions, each lasting a little over a week. Every time, we visit each village to check up on existing projects, help with any work that needs to be done, and teach the techniques in new areas. Damy comes with us to the villages that are his responsibility, and Maka comes with us to his. The number of villages and hamlets we visit gradually increases as time goes on. With the help of Damy and Maka, by the time I leave, the projects have spread to six new inland villages and are rapidly expanding. We stay in each village for one or two days, depending on the quantity of work that needs to be done. To get from one village to another we hike for hours on the small paths connecting them.

I enjoy our hikes, not only as a chance to observe the countryside but also as the only time I have to myself. I feel very privileged to be able to spend time in the bush as the only *vazaha*, surrounded by local Malagasy. It is exciting to be welcomed into tiny homes to sit on woven reed mats on the floor, to eat with families from communal plates, and to make it my challenge to improve my Malagasy speaking skills with every day that passes. However, it can also become tiring always to be the *vazaha*, the one who sticks out, the one who makes children run away in fear, the one people look at in awe, the one people see as from a different world. As we walk from one village to the next in single file, it gives me time away from the constant attention and the calls of "Salama, vazaha!" Once in a while, it is nice to be alone with my thoughts.

I also appreciate our hikes as a time to converse with Latena, Damy, and Maka. They often point out plants and animals to me along the way and explain their uses. They also discuss the daily life of people in the bush, providing me with many insights into local culture and history. Mulling over this information helps me to understand what kind of work is really needed in this area, and why some projects are neglected or become a source of conflict. It also reinforces my respect for the people in the bush, who are able to live from day to day because of their vast knowledge of how to make use of the natural resources surrounding them.

COW BANKS

Latena explains to me that *zebu*, the Malagasy humped cow, is the bank account of the bush. When someone has a bit of money saved up, he will buy a couple of chickens and raise their chicks. When he has enough chickens, he will exchange them for a sow. He will breed his sow and begin to raise the young piglets. When he has enough pigs, he will sell or trade them for a *zebu*. He will keep the *zebu* for a time of need. If someone in the family dies and needs a traditional, elaborate Malagasy funeral, or if someone gets sick and must be taken to the clinic in the faraway town, or if none of his crops survive and he has no money to buy food for his family, he can sell his *zebu* and use the money to fulfil his need. It is his insurance. The larger a man's herd of *zebu* is, the richer and more respected he is. No matter what unpredictable circumstances arise, he and his family will survive. He can afford a bride price, a funeral, a doctor, perhaps even education for his children. The savings of the Malagasy peasants graze their way through the hillsides, herded by small boys strumming rough, home-made wooden mandolins.

While Malagasy always try to show off their wealth so that they will be respected, I am constantly trying to downplay mine. When people ask me how much my shoes cost, how much my camera cost, how much my pocket knife cost, trying to gauge my wealth, I feel reluctant to say "about as much as you make in a year," widening to an even greater extent the gulf between us in their estimation. Eventually, I realize it makes more sense to put it into context instead of giving a specific price. These shoes cost a day's wage. My camera cost me two days' wages. My pocket knife was a gift, but it is worth about two hours of work. At this kind of explanation, people nod in understanding.

I realize frequently how incredibly wealthy I am not only here but compared to most people on earth. The Malagasy people I know use every cent of their wages to feed their families, and still it is often not enough. In Madagascar, both in the bush and in Fort Dauphin, I am often expected to pay for things for others—drinks, food, transportation—because everyone knows that I am able to. It is true, I am able to. I always find it difficult to decide where to draw the line. I say I am against poverty and inequality, so I should be generous and share my wealth; that is a practical action I can carry out. But how can I explain that I need to save up a bit, too, that I have student loans to pay off, that when I return to Canada I will be flat broke and without a job, that the amounts I pay for rent and food and transportation back *andafy* (abroad) are more than they can imagine?

SIKELYKELY

Back in Fort Dauphin, problems with the aquaculture project begin when Roly and I start to construct our own pond at Lanirano, the land just outside of Fort Dauphin owned by Azafady and used as a training and demonstration site. I want to begin aquaculture at Lanirano before bringing it to the bush. This will allow us to learn the technique ourselves before trying to teach it in small villages where people will depend on its success. Although the terrain at Lanirano is flat and sandy, less appropriate for a fishpond than the land in the bush, a government aquaculture specialist assures us that because of the constant water flow through the land we should not have any problems.

However, as the dry season comes upon us, the deep, rushing stream gradually dries up. We are forced to dig much deeper than we had originally planned, as well as to deepen the entire channel from the in-flowing lake to the basin. This seemingly never-ending project is carried out with spades, one wheelbarrow, and a couple of buckets. Since no one will be arriving after me to continue the project, I feel determined to at least finish the pond at Lanirano before my internship is completed. Sometimes as Roly and I stand thigh deep in muddy water, bringing one shovelful at a time up from the bottom of the pond, I wonder desperately whether all our effort will end up a waste and a failure. Often I ask myself why, exactly, I had felt ambitious enough to start this kind of a project. Why couldn't I have chosen something else, something simpler?

Perhaps because when I first arrived I did not realize that everything takes at least ten times longer in Madagascar than in Canada. Roly often tells me, when I am concerned about the pond, that my thinking is too *vazaha*. I want everything to be *fa vita amzoa*, already finished now, but in reality everything happens *sikelykely*, little by little. I try to relax and think like a Malagasy. Anything worth doing takes time. You must slip into the slow, constant rhythm of life and work patiently. Nothing is sure; you can only work hard and hope for the best.

CASSAVA

Although rice is the traditional Malagasy staple food, the true staple in the bush is cassava. Cassava is easier to grow than rice, cheaper to buy in the market, and fills the stomach more efficiently. It is a root, a heavy, tasteless starch, with the bonus ability to leach calcium. Cassava is not a food to be eaten slowly and savoured; rather it is fuel that enables you to go on working until your next meal. That being said, I do not really mind eating cassava. In fact, I even like it. Whenever I say so, however, my Malagasy hosts laugh. Silly *vazaha*. You do not *like* cassava; you just *eat* it. You like it because it is food, and therefore to be appreciated and not taken for granted. But you do not like it because of its taste. Cassava is not a taste; it is an inevitable and necessary part of life.

Everywhere in the bush I see cassava plants growing, boys pushing chopped pieces of already-harvested cassava branches into the soil to sprout into new plants, women walking straight-backed with wrapped bundles of the brown roots balanced on their heads. In front of many houses, cassava roots are spread out to dry on *tsihy*, the all-purpose mats woven from sisal or similar plants. Peeled to display their snow-white insides, the cassava roots contrast strangely with the rich colours of their surroundings, making them look naked and helpless.

While discussing the Sustainable Livelihoods vegetable gardens with Latena I stress the importance of growing legumes, not only vegetables, both as a source of protein and in order to enrich the soil. Latena tells me that people in this area used to grow peanuts and many different varieties of beans, but several years ago there was a bad drought that killed all the plants. Since then, people have grown only cassava and rice. In the market they can buy beans and peanuts grown elsewhere but seldom do. They are unwilling to spend money on beans when they can fill their bellies more cheaply with cassava. Beans have become the food of the rich, or for special occasions.

A few people still do grow legumes in the villages we visit. Whenever Latena sees bean or peanut plants he points them out to me, knowing that it will make me happy. He helps me explain to Damy and Maka why these crops are so important. He tells them that legumes *mangery*, or defecate, in the soil to make it richer. Apologetically, he tells me, "I know it is not exactly right, but they will understand it if I explain it in this way." It is a good way to explain it, I reassure him. Latena is a master at explaining, encouraging, convincing.

Damy tells Latena and me that everything in the bush is backward. Instead of growing crops to sell in town, even the basic staples of rice and cassava are now imported to the bush from town. When we come to the bush from Fort Dauphin, we must bring food supplies with us to eat and to share with our hosts. People in the bush are eager to enter the market economy, but as they ease out of pure subsistence farming they are becoming dependent on the outside world.

Damy the philosopher has a theory about how everything got turned on its head. He thinks that people spend too much time and energy making *toaky gasy*, the local moonshine rum made from distilled sugarcane, rather than on growing crops. Almost everyone in the bush produces *toaky gasy* because of the quick profit it brings. They sell it in the market but then, because they have not taken the time to grow enough food to feed their families, they are forced to use the money they earn to buy basic food supplies imported from elsewhere.

RESY

The word *resy* can mean hungry, or famine. The time of year at the end of the dry season is the *resy*. Maka and I are teaching a group of people in a village hamlet about gardening. Men, women, and children have all gathered to help and to watch. The children have red-tinged hair and their ribs stick out visibly. The babies, tied to their mothers' backs with *lamba hoany*, seem subdued as they stare out at us with eyes too large for their faces. It is nearing the end of the *resy*, and the people are tired of telling their stomachs to stop demanding food that they are unable to provide.

As we dig up the fresh soil and mix in manure, the threatening clouds suddenly open and we are caught in a torrential downpour. Excited, everyone runs back to someone's house to wait for the worst to pass. We crowd into the hut and sit on the floor in every available space. The rain pounds down on the roof and we watch the ground turn to mud outside the open doorway. As we settle in and find the most comfortable position possible, someone leaves the house to dash through the pouring rain and pick a branch from a nearby lychee tree. Our host passes the branch, laden with fruit, to Maka and me. It is Malagasy *fomba*, or custom, to offer guests food or drink when they enter your home.

I hear a few of the women talking among themselves in hushed voices. "Do you have any rice?"

"No, do you?"

"No. Is there any somewhere in the village?"

"No, there isn't any left."

"Is there any cassava, then?"

"No, no cassava, either."

"What will we offer them as food?"

"I don't know; there is nothing."

During the *resy*, even cassava is in short supply. Latena has described to me how people dig up the roots of a broad-leafed plant that grows besides streams and rivers. The root is poisonous, but if it has been soaked for a week before it is eaten it won't cause too much of a stomach ache. They eat green bananas, cooked like cassava. They eat anything they can find and wait for the rains to come and bring new life. In the meantime, the women talk quietly, trying to think of an appropriate gift for us, their guests.

It is one of the situations when I am not sure if it would be rude in Malagasy *fomba* to say anything, but I feel compelled to, either way. "No," I insist, "the lychees are already a good gift. The lychees are very good. Thank you."

In the end, that is all they offer us because that is all they have. The rain quiets and we go back outside to the newly moistened turned earth, push tiny seeds into the ground, cover them gently, and hope for their growth.

THIS LAND IS BEAUTIFUL

Ebiandry is a tiny village nestled into the foothills, lush and green in contrast with the deforested surroundings and watered by rushing streams. We are welcomed by the village president, a feeble old man with snow-white hair and a hacking cough who still manages to exude nothing but solemn dignity. I know that I am in the presence of a true chief. The entire village is his clan, or extended family. He invites us into his home, and we enter and sit on the floor. His wife steps into the hut with a bowl of freshly harvested honeycomb dripping with honey and another heaped with rice, and places them on the floor for us to share. She nods, smiling at our thanks, and leaves as quietly as she came in.

The president tells us proudly that in contrast to many of the surrounding villages that depend on supplies from the exterior, he has never had to buy food for his family. He and his entire family are still completely self-sufficient. The land gives them everything they need, he tells us. They must simply be willing to work hard to benefit from its riches. He knows he will not live much longer, but his sons are also determined to live from the land, not to be dependent on anyone.

As the president is speaking to us, one of his sons joins us and sits in the doorway of his father's hut, a *lamba hoany* wrapped around his shoulders to keep out the early morning chill. He looks out at the forested hillsides surrounding us, his home, and I hear him say quietly, reverently, "This land is beautiful."

FORESTS

On my last trip to the bush I convince Maka that I do not mind climbing a steep slope or picking leeches off my legs, so he takes us on a shortcut between two villages, up and over a hill, instead of by the path all the way around that we usually take. Our trail goes into untouched forest, one of the few patches left in this area. I wonder if it is because of the steepness of the slope that it has never been cleared.

We climb up and up, higher and higher, under the moist shade of the forest cover. We are knee high to the huge, majestic trees, climbing through a diverse collection of lush plants, mostly endemic to Madagascar. The most dramatic difference inside the forest is the sound. Birds sing in the trees, insects chirp and buzz in the bushes, water rushes in little streams. We clamber along wet, moss-covered, slippery rocks. I realize sadly that this fertile oasis of life is what much of Madagascar once looked like.

Finally, we mount the summit and start our descent beside a stream rushing down the hillside. We move carefully and slowly over the slippery rocks and through dense plant growth. "We are almost there," Maka encourages us. He has been concerned for me throughout the hike.

Abruptly, we burst into a clearing where the traces of recent slash and burn are evident. Charred, toppled tree trunks litter the hard, sun-baked, charcoal-covered earth. The clearing lies naked, a bite taken from the surrounding forest. A dirt path trails away down to a nearby village. There is no more birdsong, no comforting shade. The sun beats down on our heads and shoulders.

Maka is pleased. "Now it will be easier to walk," he encourages us happily. I follow him down the path, thinking sadly that no matter how many tree seedlings we plant, we will never be able to re-create the life-filled forest from which we have just emerged. And even our extension worker, Maka, does not realize the tragedy of this loss.

We wake up one day as the sun rises, to plant trees in Maka's village. We dig up the baby seedlings from the nursery where they have been planted and carefully place them in baskets. A few men from the families of Maka and the village president work with Latena and me, and some children from the village have also joined us. We carry the baskets to the reforestation site a little way outside the village, where early morning mist spreads in sheets over the long grass.

We get organized.... Some people are hole diggers, others are seedling carriers, and others, myself included, are the planters who tuck the seedlings into their new homes. Shy little girls carry the seedlings from the baskets to the holes, watching me quietly with their dark eyes and sometimes even returning my smiles. The boys are the most eager with the shovels, showing off by digging as fast as they can. They encourage each other—"Alefa, malakalaky!" (Let's go, faster!)—and send quick sideways glances in my direction to see my reaction, grins flashing across their faces.

Two hours later, we have finished. The seedlings stand nestled in the ground, hidden in the deep grasses. I stand for a moment to look out over the field bathed in soft morning light before returning to the village with the others to share a communal breakfast of rice and boiled sweet potato leaves. I hope that roaming *zebu* and occasional fires will stay away long enough that these trees can grow tall and re-clothe the land that has been stripped bare. I know the forest that once stood here can never grow back, but I hope that these trees will provide needed resources for Maka's village. When every stick of wood used to cook or build with must be collected from farther away than the one the day before, life increasingly becomes a struggle for survival.

MARO THE MAGNET

Once, I tell Latena that I feel unnecessary during our trips to the bush. He knows the language and culture and politics of the situation and is more than competent by himself. I tell him I feel as though there is no point to my being there. It is a wonderful experience for me, but of no use whatsoever to the people in the bush.

"No, it is good that you are here," he tells me earnestly.

"Why?" I ask, eager to discover a reason I have not thought of. The issue has been bothering me for some time. If Latena thinks I should be here, then surely there is a good reason.

"Because if only Malagasy come to a village with an idea for a project, it is hard to get people's attention. The people in the bush are busy trying to survive, and they cannot risk trying new ideas unless they know they will work. But if a *vazaha* comes, they will listen. When a *vazaha* comes to the bush, it is easy to get everyone together to talk to them about a project. As soon as the *vazaha* comes into the village, the whole village will assemble to look at her. So you do not need to call a meeting to get everyone together."

I laugh. It is true, of course. Every time I walk into a village I immediately have a curious entourage surrounding me. I also know that people see the Sustainable Livelihoods projects as more of a priority when they know that a *vazaha* comes regularly to assess their progress. That is my use, then. The Canadian International Development Agency has funded me to come to the other side of the world so that I can serve as a magnet, an efficient village assembler.

"Why are you laughing?" Latena asks curiously. "It is true!"

"Yes, I know it is true," I assure him.

Maro the magnet.

That is an acceptable purpose for a six-month internship as a recently graduated student, I decide. But one day, somehow, somewhere, I hope to gain skills and knowledge that can be of use here and in other similar places. I want to be able to bring some truly useful gift, however small, to these people who have given me so much.

FISHPONDS AND CYCLONES

Back in Lanirano, we do finally complete the pond, only days before I leave. I leave my research material and a proposal for the continuation of the project in the bush in the hope that someone will eventually take over the project. A few months after I return to Canada, Brett sends me an email telling me that the land at Lanirano has been hit hard by the cyclones that struck Madagascar shortly after I left. He writes apologetically that the fishpond, as well as everything around it, flooded completely and was washed out in the torrential rains. However, there is good news, too. A potential volunteer who has studied aquaculture is interested in continuing the project in the bush.

More than anything, I am glad to receive his news. I find it ironic that the pond we struggled so hard to keep from drying out was destroyed by floods. But spending time with people who live at a subsistence level impressed upon me that humans are vulnerable and unable to control their environment, a fact easily forgotten in the West, where we live buffered by technology. And an aquaculture specialist interested in continuing the project is very good news. What is important to me is that the project eventually benefits people in the bush.

The fishpond project confirms for me the importance of patience in development work, as well as continuity. An internship of six months is not enough to begin a new project, at least not if there is no one to continue it afterward. It takes longer than six months just to begin to discover how things work locally, what is considered culturally appropriate, and what impact the cycle of the seasons has on people's lives. I am not ready to co-ordinate and complete a project as a *vazaha* fresh off the plane from *andafy*, the Malagasy word for everywhere other than Madagascar, collectively a different, unknown world.

SUSTAINABLE LIVELIHOODS

Shortly before leaving Madagascar, while following Damy and Latena along a trail between villages, I ponder the effectiveness of our work. Although some of the Sustainable Livelihoods projects do well and provide people with food and income, others are neglected. Our visits introduce us to local conflicts, things not working out as planned, and people looking for free handouts from *vazahas* ... challenges that anyone working in development has to face. However, more and more people are adopting the projects as their own, planting gardens and trees, harvesting honey more sustainably and easily than from their traditional hives, and brainstorming new ideas for projects. Are their lives better than before?

In the face of the powerful forces of natural resource depletion and the rapid diffusion of the cash economy, change in these villages is inevitable. The question is, what is the best way to change? What new ideas should be combined with traditional methods to improve the health and well-being of people in the bush? I hope that Azafady's work will lessen people's constant struggle for survival. I hope that Malagasy and *vazaha* working in partnership, meshing their different skills and knowledge, can improve the local standard of living in a sustainable way. I hope that my role as a "magnet" has served to teach skills that will benefit the people who learn them. But sometimes I wonder who has learned the most over these past six months: the people I have met in the bush, or me?

In the bush, although I have seen poverty more extreme than I had ever encountered before, I find the majority of the people I meet to be happy and skilled at using the resources available to them. I enjoy being in a place where everything is completely fresh and from its source. I watch people harvesting and drying and roasting the coffee I drink. I observe people drying and weaving sisal and a local plant called *mahampy* to make mats and baskets like the ones I use. I have seen people plant, thin, and harvest rice, dry it, pound it with a mortar and pestle, sift through it by hand to pick out husks and stones, and boil it over a wood fire for my meals. Seeing the entire process behind each meal and tool makes me appreciate them far more than I otherwise would. A part of me dreads returning to North America where, in comparison, everything seems rushed, wasteful, and isolated from its source.

It is true that nothing from filling a *taxi-brousse* to improving sustainable livelihoods happens quickly and efficiently in Madagascar. But if you choose to accept this fact, you begin to appreciate the creative ways in which people use the resources around them. In Madagascar, I have met people who are unable to read and write but who know the names and uses for countless plant and animal species. I have met people who know how to survive even when there is drought and even when there is flooding and even when they have eight children to feed. Maybe what I appreciate most of all is the people I know who have nothing but cassava to eat three times a day, but who still invite me into their tiny huts to share it with them.

TWO WORLDS

One night in the bush I have a dream. I am walking down my parents' street, lined by tall, majestic trees. I look up into the treetops and discover to my surprise that they are mango and lychee and avocado trees. I had never noticed that these fruits grew so near to where my parents live. I continue walking down the street, and turn to enter the house. I am returning from a long voyage, possibly from Madagascar. I enter the house quietly and walk along the hall, through the dining room, and into the kitchen. I stand in the doorway observing the room. The wooden cupboards line the walls in a precise row. The deep red counter is perfectly straight and flat, arranged in a U that most conveniently provides a place for appliances and utensils. I stare, as if for the first time, at the high ceiling and square walls and co-ordinated colours.

My sister, Anna, is standing in front of the counter with her back to me, busy with my father's new espresso machine. I study the espresso machine, shining silver and black, complex, precise, thoughtfully designed. Plugged in to run on the never-ending source of electricity that feeds into this house. Every part of the machine is designed with a function. Here is where you pour the water. This part steams the milk. Here is where you put the ground coffee. This is what you press it down with.

Anna turns to look at me, and smiles. She does not seem surprised in the least to see me, despite my long absence. "I'm just making myself a cup of coffee," she says. "Would you like one, too?"

"Sure," I say. "Thank you."

And then a rooster crows particularly loudly just outside the thin wall, and I wake up suddenly. I am looking up at the inside of a thatched roof about six feet above my head. I slowly drift back into reality and soak in my surroundings. I am lying on the floor of Damy's house on a woven mat, wrapped in a thin blanket like a cocoon. My sweater is folded and tucked under my head as a pillow. On my right lies Latena, similarly cocoonlike, still sleeping, beside the wall of vertical palm branches. His head is against one wall, and his feet almost reach the opposite end of the house. Two of Damy's children and one of his nephews slept in a row to the left of me, but when I turn my head they have already left the house to go about their work. When all five of us were lying down on the floor to sleep, we filled the entire house from side to side. Damy and his wife and the baby slept in the little cooking house next door to give us room.

The rooster crows again and I yawn, untangle myself from my blanket, and get up. I slide the palm-branch door sideways and duck to exit by the low doorway, step down onto the ground, and slip into my flip-flops. My watch says it is five-thirty. The morning is fresh and cool although the sun is already bright. Smoke curls up from the cooking house where Damy's daughter is cooking over the fire. His son and nephew are hoeing cassava in the field beside the house. My dream still vividly floats through my mind as I take in the morning smells and sounds. I imagine describing it to someone here. "I just had a dream. I was walking down the road to my parents' house, and it was lined with mango and lychee and avocado trees. I walked into the house. My sister was in the kitchen, making coffee. She asked me if I would like a cup, and I said yes I would, thank you."

And then my mind flashes to what that description would mean to whomever I told it to here in the bush. I imagine the scene. I walk along a narrow path lined, not surprisingly, with commonly found fruit trees. I come into a clearing where I see a tiny palm-branch hut. Ducking to enter the hut, I see a young girl squatting beside a smoky fire. Her hair is braided into tiny braids and twisted into two matching buns over her ears. She is wearing a torn and dirty dress that is too small for her. She stirs fresh coffee in a soot-stained pot balanced over the fire. Earlier, she had picked the coffee berries from the tree, spread them on a mat to dry, pounded them with her wooden mortar and pestle, and roasted the beans over a fire. Now, stirring the hot liquid sweetened with cane juice, she turns with a smile and asks me if I would like some. When I say I would, she dips a small tin cup into the pot and hands it to me. I squat on the dirt floor as I drink to prevent my head from brushing against the thatched roof of the hut.

This scene collides in my mind with the still-lingering memory of my dream. The gleaming espresso machine and the smoky fire spin together. My sister and a thin black girl in a dust-coloured dress take turns smiling at me over their shoulders. The contrast between the two worlds strikes me more forcefully than it ever has before. I shake my head to try to stop the vivid images.

Latena emerges from the hut, his tall frame stooped over to fit through the doorway. He slips into his sandals and walks toward me, smiling. "Natory soa hanoa?" (Did you sleep well?), he asks.

"Eka" (Yes), I respond, smiling, and follow him into the cooking hut. We squat on the dirt floor and watch Damy's daughter stirring a pot of coffee over the fire.

7

Travelling to El Otro Lado

Simon Yale Strauss

I think it is best to begin the story by going backward.

It is January 2006. I am sitting at my desk in the small, eminently comfortable house that my parents own in downtown Toronto, poring over the results from my fieldwork and still a full eight months away from completing my master's degree in human geography. Pages and pages of notes sit before me, taken during a number of interviews I had with *campesinos*—literally, people of the field—over a few weeks in Queretaro, a state in the mountains of central Mexico. I pull out the top questionnaire in the pile and pop the corresponding tape into the mini-recorder. A croaky voice, which it always takes me a second to recognize as my own, clears its throat and asks in hesitant Spanish, "Bueno, cómo se llama usted?"

This particular interview is with a man in his midforties named Ramiro Gonzalez. As with all of my interviews, I had approached his house, explained that I was a Canadian student doing a social study in the area, and been offered a seat. As the interview began, Ramiro sent a child out to pick me a bag of small, dry peaches as a gift, the only product that seems to grow in abundance on the increasingly unproductive land of the Mexican central highlands. Through nearly fifty prepared questions and a few that were ad libbed in conversation, Ramiro related to me the history of his life in the mountains, how work and good land had been scarce recently and how most of the young people left the town right after high school to go to *el otro lado* (the other side), to find jobs in the United States. More often, he said despairingly, than they stayed make a life for themselves here.

At the end of the interview, now with the charcoal smell of cooking smoke deep in my nostrils and my clothing, I turn the tables for a second, as manners and my training require me to, and ask him if he has any questions for me. Though some *campesinos* shy at the prospect of asking the *gringo* a question, not feeling they would have anything to ask, or perhaps never having been given the opportunity before, Ramiro is not discouraged by my education or background and has no qualms about asking me what I am doing there, in a place that for me is *el otro lado*.

"So you're here for what, exactly? Who was it that sent you?"

I explain again that the process is part of my thesis, an investigation mostly for my own interest, and perhaps to aid in the planning of sustainable development strategies in the area where he lives. In retrospect, I should probably just have begun with "It's to forward my career" (which, incidentally, is a response most people are happier with), though I know that that wouldn't be completely right.

"Are you paid to come?" he asks.

"Yes and no" is my response, as the substantial government loans that I took out will have to be paid back when I am done. It is at this point that I receive an almost audible sideways look from Ramiro, a look I have got used to in the past international work that I have done. It is the kind of look that asks why I would come all this way and (often) pay so much, just to find out how things work in this little town that no one has ever taken any interest in. *Estás loco*? Am I crazy? Most young people living there do not even want to stay. What is in this impoverished, economic-refugee–producing side of the world for someone like me?

And with *estás loco* in mind, I begin a search for an answer to the question that Ramiro posed with his sideways glance, the question of *el otro lado*. Mexicans have been migrating to El Norte for decades, often out of dire necessity, looking for economic opportunities that are not available to them in their own country—so much so that the amount of money sent back to relatives living in Mexico, estimated in the billions of dollars annually, outweighs the nation's yearly agricultural output. North Koreans do the same to China, much as North Africans flood the shores of France and Spain, hoping to provide for their families. What is it about us, as inhabitants of the Western world, that makes us want to reverse that flow and head out, some for years at a time, to the most forgotten and derelict ends of the Earth to volunteer our time? What causes us to leave our homes, our comfort zones, and head out into what is often unknown and potentially dangerous? The answer, in most cases, is certainly not economic (ask anyone earning an NGO salary), and usually far from necessary. It is also not so easy to describe. For me at least, it has been clarified by three distinct overseas experiences: the fieldwork in Mexico (summer 2005), being a teacher's assistant in Panama (winter 2005), and volunteering in Rwanda (summer and fall 2003).

In March 2005, I was a teacher's assistant for a field course, one component of a larger program in which twenty-five students from McGill University spent three months living, working, and studying in Panama. As part of my duties, I provided the logistics for a week-long road trip across the country, stopping at dams, plantations, and mines along the way to learn how Panamanians are using their resources and how they are trying to mitigate the ways in which they affect the environment. By the end of the week, which at times felt more like a marathon of emotional and physical endurance than an undergraduate course, we students returned exhausted but with a deep appreciation for the value of seeing environmental issues through the eyes of those living with them, not something easily gained from the classroom. In the days following the course, as the students wrote their final reports and made preparations to leave Panama City to travel or return home, I reflected on my experiences and sent out an email with my parting thoughts.

"Think back to all the people you grew up with. How many of them have never left their own country? How many have never left their province or state? How many are still in the same city where they were born? Very few people in the world have the opportunity to do what you did, to see another part of the world as you did, to be so far out of their comfort zone. Along the way, you've learned that what is most interesting about the world is the people in it, since wherever you go will bear the marks of humanity. So I say: don't waste this chance. When you go home, talk to everyone you can about your experiences here—quell their fears, dispel their misconceptions, and inspire them to do the same. And always, wherever you go in the world, make sure you talk to the people there. Whether you're beginning your master's, working construction, continuing your travels, or going home and relaxing for a while, remember that there's something to be learned every day from the people that you meet. Get their life stories, and use them to learn about how the world works. Approach new situations with curiosity, open-mindedness, and just the right amount of naïveté. Become a good listener, if you're not one already."

In reading over these words today, I wonder how condescending they might seem. I certainly wasn't trying to speak down to the students, though some may have taken it that way. These were lessons that I had only begun to appreciate toward the end of the course, and as I sent the email I was taken by the fact that I had felt the confidence and authority to say them to others. I was also surprised by just how strongly I had come to believe in them. Herein lies perhaps the first answer to the question posed to me by Ramiro and the other Mexican farmers I met during my fieldwork: We do it because we want to understand how the world works. We know that the world is deeply affected by humans, and in turn we are deeply interested in the humans who inhabit it. We are curious, we are idealistic, and often, we think we can make a difference somehow. We are also lucky enough to have the luxury to do such things and effect such changes, to journey to our own personal *otro lado*.

To go back further still means addressing the experience that solidified these ideas for me in the first place. In late February 2003, I was offered a six-month placement with a Canadian-based NGO called Right to Play (RTP). The organization sends volunteers, mostly men and women in their twenties and early thirties, to refugee camps and other highly marginal areas to organize sport and play programs for children and teenagers. During my interview, I mentioned that I would like to go to Central America, given that I could speak Spanish and would probably be most useful there. To say that I had not really considered Africa as a travel destination would be an understatement— being the young, upper-middle-class idealist that I was, I knew that the world was my oyster and had already made a mental checklist of the regions I had an interest in seeing: Latin America and Southeast Asia, among others. "The dark continent," as it was once known, did not even register. A few days after my interview, I received an email announcing my acceptance and placement in, of all places, a camp in Rwanda.

My parents gasped (albeit internally). My mother said I couldn't go, though at twenty-six, I knew she couldn't really stop me. My father, a journalist and Google-holic, found pictures of the place I would be staying. The town was called Kibuye and was situated on the shores of Lake Kivu, bordering the Democratic Republic of the Congo (DRC). "It doesn't look so bad," he said, seeing the idyllic photos of the one hotel in town, though he admitted only after my return home that he was absolutely terrified for me. For my part, with only two weeks to prepare between the acceptance and the beginning of training, I had little time to feel any sense of trepidation or worry. I was invincible, I thought, and this would be an adventure like the others I had had in the past.

The months leading up to my interview with Right to Play had been difficult ones for me. Having finished my undergraduate degree in biology in 2000 and then spent a semester studying and working in Panama in early 2001, I had passed the next year and a half working at whatever jobs came up, with little direction or focus. A look at my résumé from that time is proof: database designer, costume store clerk, caterer, event promoter. I ended up moving back home with my parents in September 2002, and doing data entry for a car-share company in Toronto—again, the first job that came up.

I knew that I wanted to go abroad again. The travelling bug, once it has bit, is hard to shake for many. And my experience in the developing world had shown me that it was there that I wanted to go, to visit *el otro lado*, though without clearly defining why. In retrospect, I probably wanted to experience the same feeling of wonder, of insatiable curiosity, that I had felt on visiting Panama for the first time in 2001, that feeling of being somewhere so completely different from what I was used to, of learning a different lifestyle, of having to slow down to adjust to time in the land of *mañana*, and to get used to the unpredictability of a life in which no one respects the street signs and almost anything that is for sale can be bargained for.

During these months, I had been searching online for any number of opportunities. For North Americans with means, there is a seemingly endless list of things to apply for: just have a look at some of the major websites devoted to the subject, such as devnetjobs.org, idealist.org, or devex.com. One thing that both the developed and the developing worlds teach you is that it is not only what you know but who, and it was the who that got me in the door for my journey to Africa. My initial contact came through a friend of my mother's who worked with RTP, and I applied in December 2002. For two months I waited for a response, only hearing rumours that some restructuring was going on. Finally, in mid-February, I received word that they would like to interview me. And the rest, as I've already let on, is history.

With two weeks to prepare before training and deployment, I had scarcely enough time to get my shots and buy supplies for the trip. During the rush of preparation, it did not even occur to me to have a good look at background materials on the country—I simply asked my father if he could buy a few books about Africa that I could read once I arrived. So, packed along with a mosquito net, good waterproof boots, Lariam, and Tilley hat, was a varied selection of books that he had either heard of or found out about in his search: *A Bend in the River*, by V.S. Naipaul; *Under the Neem Tree*, by Susan Lowerre; *In the Arms of Africa: The Life of Colin M. Turnbull*, by Roy Richard Grinker; and *The Shadow of the Sun*, by Ryszard Kapuściński. These books, along with others that I would borrow from fellow expats, would provide the larger context for my experiences in Rwanda.

My training for RTP consisted of an intense week with thirty other volunteers. While most of us were Canadian, Argentina, Sweden, Australia, and Scotland were also represented. On the first day of these meetings I met the person who would influence my experience in Rwanda more than anyone else: Caroline, the woman who would be my colleague for the six-month stay. We had already sent a few emails back and forth, introducing ourselves and asking questions of one another, and I'd received an inkling of her personality. At one point, I had found out that cashing traveller's cheques might be difficult, so I passed on this bit of information to her. "I could have told you that," was the response, and it was an omen of the relationship that would prove to be the most difficult part of my stay in East Africa. At training, my suspicions were confirmed: in placing the two of us together, Right to Play had chosen two people of almost polar opposite personalities, what psychologists might term the typical Type A and Type B. While I am reserved, take my time making decisions, often look for consensus before undertaking a task, can be absentminded and disorganized, and take great pleasure in personal time, Caroline on first impression was outgoing, bubbly, sometimes quick to criticize, highly motivated and organized, and clearly in her element when surrounded by groups of people. She lived her life as an (!), while I was more of a (...). It was going to be a long trip.

And so, buoyed by the adventure of it all, though wary of our conflicting personalities, I boarded the plane with Caroline and departed from Toronto in early March 2003. I still did not really know, or had not seriously considered, why I was going. I just knew that something awaited me in this unfamiliar land, something that might help to quell my restlessness and pique my curiosity. I felt that I wanted to "help," in some abstract form of the word, to give of my time, my expertise, and my patience.

Helping, as I know now, is rarely as altruistic as it sounds, and this is perhaps a second part of the answer to Ramiro's question. We, as development workers, are the missionaries of the new millennium, venturing out to help ease the suffering of those less fortunate. While many of us are ostensibly driven by an unselfish desire to help, with perhaps no deeper faith than in that of humanity, our voyage to *el otro lado* is undertaken with the knowledge that we stand to benefit as much as, or more than, our intended recipients. With no heavenly reward in mind, we are in search of a much more pragmatic kind: to better ourselves, to expand our horizons, to improve our prospects in our personal and professional lives. As much as we hate to admit it, we are not unselfish creatures but are doing what we do partly to fulfil our internal needs as well as those of others.

RWANDA

> Imana yirirwa ahandi igataha mu Rwanda.
> (God spends the day doing good things elsewhere, but sleeps in Rwanda.)
> —*Rwandan saying*

Kibuye, as I soon found out, was a sparsely populated town of just forty-seven thousand people, slumbering on the edge of Lake Kivu, which borders the DRC. Kivu's surface houses a number of boats, many water filled and unusable; the rest are either for short tours of the lake or belong to the fishermen who make their living from its waters. Large dugouts are bound together in groups of three for stability, with huge poles protruding from either end of each boat, like antennae off some giant floating insect. During daylight, you could watch the fishermen cast their nets; at night—and they fish for most of the night—the only evidence of activity was a single lantern hung from the middle boat, easily mistaken for the light of a house at the other end of the lake.

A road winds up and down the side of surrounding cliffs, giving unexpected vistas of the blue-green water and the action along the lakeshore. Following the road on foot, you pass the beer-delivery hangar, where boats from the national brewery in the north, Gisenyi, drop off new cases of Primus and Mutzig and carry away the empties. Young children, mostly unsupervised, strip down to nakedness and plunge into the water, laughing and gurgling. Military men on their time off do the same in their boxer shorts. Women wearing colourful *pagnes* and balancing basins on their heads proceed to the shore to chat and do the laundry. A few young men prefer fly-fishing with bamboo rods. Antiquated ships—now relics from another time—have become rusted playgrounds for children and birds alike.

Our first two months in Rwanda were filled with seemingly endless evenings. There had been problems with our work visas, meaning we could not legally visit the refugee camp where we would be working, and we had yet to make many good friendships among the other expats. Having little to do meant that I could spend ample time walking around and exploring the banks of the lake and observing the activities in and around it. In the long evenings, often after another frustrating day stuck in the office and following our nightly cribbage matches, I began to write. Not in any kind of regular journal, as I had done as a child, but on the laptop RTP had provided before we left Toronto.

My writing took the form of extended email updates home, and reached a mailing list that included about two hundred family members, friends, and acquaintances whom I had met and stayed in touch with over the years. While I had not intended for the updates to become epics, I realized that writing became my form of expression, of catharsis, of communication, in a land so devoid of the normal and the trite of North American life. Every day was an experience in patience and understanding, and the best way I found to make sense of it all was to create an open journal of sorts, pre-dating the now ubiquitous blogs that choke the arteries of the Internet. These writings provided a framework that now allows me to address some of the answers to Ramiro's query.

CULTURAL ADAPTATION

Going to black Africa[1] meant losing any anonymity that I had had in Canada. Everywhere, we were stared at as if we were creatures from another planet, not simply another part of the world. Cries of "Muzungu! muzungu!" the Swahili and Kinyarwandan equivalent of "whitey," followed us down the street. Children walked alongside us and asked for money, waved, or smiled. Adults usually just stared or turned away. I remember thinking to myself that this must be what celebrity is like, what Wayne Gretzky or Pamela Anderson or Bryan Adams must feel when walking down the street. You can never be at ease: you are constantly ogled and become the topic in someone's daily gossip. The scene played out in my head.

"Guess who I saw today?"

"Who?"

"The new *muzungu*!"

"No way! Another one?" Raucous peals of laughter.

Along with this alienation was the feeling that my being in Rwanda as a development worker smacked of latent colonialism. We expats were chauffeured around by local drivers in our huge Land Rovers as if on safari, looking out onto the poverty and desolation lining the roads while people outside looked at the *muzungu* riding stoically along on uneven mountain roads. Children would jump up out of ditches alongside the road and scream as if Santa Claus had just flown by on his shiny white four-wheeled sled. I thought to myself that my own ancestors, only two or three generations before, had been living in the European version of this poverty. It became impossible not to question this obvious difference in wealth and opportunities, and I was forced to reflect on why it was my lot to be on one side of the window and not the other. Was I really worthy of the choices that had been laid out at my feet almost since my birth? Conversely, I also started asking myself what, with such profound differences, it is that we all share. What is it that makes us all human?

Most obviously, I thought, it must be language, and the intricacies of communication that come with it. Among other things, what we as humans share is a desire to communicate, to be understood, to share knowledge. Although my purchase of the *Lonely Planet* Swahili phrasebook proved less useful than I had hoped (most Rwandans converse in the local language, Kinywarwanda), the lessons on grammar and pronunciation it contained allowed me to pick up Kinywarwanda more rapidly. Speaking the language began with asking a friend how to say something, then writing it down phonetically as I heard it. My early vocabulary consisted of the basics—*mulaho* (hello to strangers or after a long absence), *amakuru* (how are you?), *nmeza* (good, fine), *pilipili* (local hot sauce), *buracosé* (thank you), *araru mutieho* (see you tomorrow), *witwa nde* (what's your name?), and so on. Most attempts at using the language were met with a smile, as people did seem to appreciate my trying

Even learning these basics was a challenge, however, given that they required a new set of sounds, or at least familiar sounds used in new ways. When I did finally get hold of a dictionary, I found that words are indeed spelled phonetically, thanks to the missionary zeal of Bible translation,[2] with pronunciations close to Spanish or Italian: the *r* and the *l* are so close that Sara, a Canadian friend working for the United Nations High Commissioner for Refugees (UNHCR) in Kigali, learned to answer to the local version of her name, Sala. Despite this, many words begin with two consonants (*mneliwe, nde*), sometimes three (*nbweza*), and sounds are often swallowed or downplayed so that their phonetic spellings do not always correspond, at least to an ear trained in the Germanic and Romance languages. Picking up new words was thus more an exercise in aping what I heard than in actually understanding the language.

Luckily for me, children often make the best teachers, as they perhaps have the extra patience and are more wont to see the inherent humour in teaching a foreigner. In trying to fill some of the time during my first months, I decided to head down to the stadium in town and play with the gaggles of children who regularly hung out there. As they did seemingly everywhere in the country, they ran up and surrounded me like a mini-paparazzi, wanting to say hello, feel the novelty of my hairy forearms, and have some adult attention. I assumed, perhaps too quickly, that most were street kids, given the state of their clothing and the fact that they were not in school. So what does one do for conversation with a nearly insurmountable language barrier?

I pointed to my eyes, and said, "Kinyarwanda? Kinyarwanda?"

"Amaso," one eventually replied, shyly, finally understanding my gesticulations. I repeated the word, to huge smiles on the part of everyone. Ears? *Amatwi*, they told me in unison. Now they got the idea. Hair? *Umusatsi*. Nose? *Izuru*. Mouth? *Umunwa*. Teeth? *Amenyo*. And so on. To keep track, along with the basic phrases in my notebook, I included a labelled diagram of a child covered, head to foot, with the terms these children gave me, on various days, for whatever objects were close at hand: grass, sun, boys, girls, football, stones. Though I could barely string a sentence together, I still proudly told people one of my favourite words in Kinyarwanda: *ikambambiri*. It seemed like quite a mouthful just to say "flip-flop."

From these baby steps into the realm of communication, I was also initiated into the subtleties of body language, a much more problematic and culturally loaded domain, much like learning an entirely different language on its own. Being in a largely Christian country, I did not have to worry about many of the issues that colleagues in Muslim Africa had to take into account: men and women can greet each other and converse in public, and eye contact does not seem to be a huge point of contention. Ironically, I found, for a place where homosexuality "does not exist" (as we were informed on a few occasions), public intimacy between men is acceptable and indeed customary. It is not uncommon to have your hand held in a handshake for an entire conversation, to see a man sit down on his (male) friend's lap and lay his arm around the sitter's neck, or to see two friends walking down the street holding hands (all the more striking when it was two soldiers in full combat gear). As a man myself, I realized how much this intimacy was lacking in North American life, and how I had built up a mental wall to bar other men from entering my personal space. Slowly, I let my guard down over the six months of my stay and eventually relished the bonding that this closeness allowed.

Finally, I realized that, as different and difficult as all these minutiae of language are, there are certain ways to communicate across all cultures. As I walked into the local market one day, I found myself distracted by a new food being offered and accidentally hit my head on one of the stalls (made for people on average much shorter than I am). The reaction? Laughter, of course. At a coach training session the following week, I taught our volunteers one of my favourite schoolyard games, known as Ha-Goo. An Alaskan Tlingit game, the point is to make someone on the other team laugh without touching them in any way. The utter hilarity of seeing grown men and women, usually reserved though warm, making faces, sounds, and dancing à la John Cleese was enough to send the entire room into hysterics, ending in one of those games that everyone wins. Physical humour, as I discovered, is understood by all.

WORK

My only comment upon arrival at the camp for the first time was that it had been the longest short trip I'd ever taken. The problems of refugees are many, not the least of which is that the land given to them by the host government is usually unwanted by others. The Kiziba camp was no exception. The travel time from Kibuye was only about forty minutes, but the entire trip was made along a rocky, uneven road snaking along the edge of steep, green cliffs. Though the landscape remained picturesque, I was hard pressed to remain stoically in my seat while being jostled around so vigorously.

As seen from the road, the camp was a collection of a few hundred aluminum-roofed houses and huts, aligned along a gently sloping incline. From afar, the community resembled a perfectly broken mirror spread along the side of the hill, each roof glinting in the sunlight like a shard of glass. The elementary and high school buildings were covered almost entirely with green plastic UNHCR sheeting, or tarp, and were thus easily distinguishable from their reflective neighbours.

Stepping out of our Land Rovers and into the camp for the first time had the same effect as elsewhere in the country; we were the immediate centre of attention, especially since we were the *new muzungu* and not the regular UNHCR crew. Adults, both young and old, stared, though they could not help cracking a smile when I said hello and how are you in my pidgin Kinyarwanda. Younger children saw us with a mix of fascination and reservation; as we walked along the roads, they followed behind, close enough to invade our personal space though avoiding contact. When I stopped and faced away, I felt little hands run their way along my forearm, feeling the body hair so uncharacteristic of most Africans.

The camp was made up of close to fourteen thousand Congolese refugees, the majority of whom were teenagers and young adults. Most spoke Kinyarwanda, along with a mix of French, Swahili, and Lingala. Contrary to common perceptions of refugee camps, the houses were permanent mud huts with metal roofs, some not much bigger than my bathroom at home; these were not the characteristic tents so often presented in the media back home. Everywhere were children—four-year-olds holding two-year-olds, most unaccompanied, sitting naked and dirty on the ground, noses running—crying, laughing, or playing as children would anywhere. Women walked around carrying children swathed in cloth on their backs, papoose style, so that only a brown head and pair of tiny feet poked out of the wrapping. As Carlos Ramirez, the head of UNHCR in Kibuye described it, family planning was out the window, and women were essentially baby machines, as a bigger family was thought to secure more substantial food rations. Thoughts of the "Please send your support, a child in Africa needs you" ads on TV flashed through my mind, the white spokesperson wading through a sea of shoeless villagers.

My first impressions of the camp were of shock at the destitution surrounding me, but as I spent more time there I realized that the settlement was highly organized and actually functioned more like a small village. Congolese society is essentially tribal, with each grouping of people having a *mwami* (chief), in charge of representing them and, in the past at least, of distributing land. In the case of the camp, at the lowest level of organization every ten houses formed a *nyumba kumi* (literally "ten houses" in Kiswahili) and had a representative. These *nyumba kumi* (also the name given to the representatives), together with the president of the camp, made up the camp council. Other councils also drew on the *nyumba kumi* system, as every set of ten houses also had a women's representative, a youth representative, an old man's (*mze*) representative, and so on. Community structures included two churches (Anglican and Catholic); a community centre and women's centre; an outdoor meeting place; kindergarten, primary, and secondary schools; job training centres; and various neighbourhoods. As food, clothing, and housing were all taken care of through the various NGOs and United Nations branches working in the camp, most people had nothing in the way of work, leading to a number of problems that we are used to hearing about in the context of First Nations reserves in Canada: lethargy, alcoholism, spousal abuse and other violence, and uncontrolled pregnancy.

The camp set-up and issues of insecurity struck me as only natural, considering what we humans are made to do. We are indelibly social creatures, hardwired to seek out the company of others to share in our joys, our sorrows, our triumphs. Millennia of living together in communities have shown us that we need some amount of political organization to maintain order and minimize conflict, and to exist happily in a small space with neighbours close at hand. With fourteen thousand of these neighbours squeezed into an area the size of a few city blocks, it would be impractical to have complete participation and consensus in order to reach decisions, so the camp was broken down into smaller and smaller units for ease of decision making and information spreading.

We humans are also task oriented and do not do well with nothing to do. Our bodies tell us to get up, get moving, till the fields, kill the boars, reproduce. Our lives must have a purpose, a meaning, a direction. We need stimulation. In refugee camps or First Nations reserves, where people have little to do and few prospects for the future, these energies are left to boil and ferment, eventually bubbling over into the familiar forms of aggression and abuse. There is no great mystery why these places are all too often breeding grounds for rebellion, violence, and unrest; people are just searching for the means to achieve normality and stability in their lives, a way to balance the need to "do" with the need to interact with others.

My working life in the camp was at once the most frustrating and the most satisfying experience I can remember. RTP's programs, based on volunteerism and aimed largely at getting younger children, women, and people with disabilities involved as much as possible, often conflicted with the local views that we should be paying people for their "work" with us and that sports were a man's domain. Our mandate also required that we set up a sports council to decide how leagues would be organized and to ensure proper representation for the various groups in the camps (young and old, men and women, disabled people). This came into direct conflict with the existing governance structure, a system already boasting a (young, male) sports representative, who needless to say was not happy about the power sharing involved.

In an attempt to assuage this tension, we tried to give a feeling of ownership of the sports council to the camp as a whole. We called a meeting for everyone who was interested and asked for candidates for each position to stand up and give a short speech about why they should be on the council. The meeting began slowly—half an hour after the starting time of 4:00 p.m., we had only thirteen attendees (all male) for twelve positions—but by 5:15, as afterschool and women's literacy programs finished and their members trickled in, we had what can only be described as a madhouse of 120 people. The *only* way to determine who would fill each position—a novel method suggested by the attendees themselves—was to have each candidate turn around after the speeches to allow the audience members to line up behind the person of their choice. It was brilliant in its simplicity. It ensured that everyone could vote only once, there was no messing around with paper and pens (also important considering high illiteracy rates), and the winners were usually easy to declare. A candidate with 80 per cent of the vote would be revealed by a quick glance at the queue leading down the hall. The active involvement of the audience also lent the event a festive air, and people celebrated each winner with a round of laughter and applause. I came home that day exhausted and hoarse, though satisfied with the community's choice of sports representatives.

Working at the camp, and indeed working in Rwanda generally, often meant keeping a degree of flexibility in our planning that is simply not done in the West. As Carlos, the UNHCR head, quipped at one point, the word *wait* actually stands for "West African Internal Time," a joke we soon discovered was all too true. In my reading, one passage stood out as especially adroit, from Kapuściński's *Shadow of the Sun*:

> We climb on to the bus and sit down. At this point there is a risk of culture clash, of collision and conflict. It will undoubtedly occur if the passenger is a foreigner who doesn't know Africa. Someone like that will start looking around, squirming, inquiring, "When will the bus leave?"
>
> "What do you mean, when?" the astonished driver will reply. "It will leave when we find enough people to fill it up."
>
> ... In practical terms, this means that if you go to a village where a meeting is scheduled for the afternoon, but find no one at the appointed spot, asking, "When will the meeting take place?" makes no sense. You know the answer: "It will take place when people come."

The European view of time is Newtonian, he notes, in that we are subject to it and must adhere to its linearity and inflexibility. If you show up late, you miss the meeting. In Africa, he goes on, it is we who influence time, and events cannot occur unless people are present. More than once, my (European) patience was tried by the (African) view of time.

During one coach training class, for example, I arrived by the scheduled 10:00 a.m. and sat down to wait for our coaches-in-training to show up. The building where we held our training sessions was a one-room mud-brick house, similar to though substantially larger than the dwellings in which everyone lived. It was equipped with the basics: four benches and a blackboard, a couple of chairs, four windows with wooden shutters, and just enough space to allow for some of the simpler games that I was to teach. Each morning, as soon as I was seen disembarking from the Land Rover, the neighbourhood children would rush to the windows of the room, eager to watch over the proceedings. I would open the latches, swing the shutters open, and almost instantaneously the sunlight that poured in was partially darkened by the multitude of curious heads, arms, and hands that would fill the window's opening.

On this particular day, I waited until 10:30, at which time Patrice, one of the trainees, arrived, sat for fifteen minutes, then asked where everyone was.

"Good question," I replied, with more than a hint of frustration in my voice.

"I'll go and get them," he said, and promptly left the room to find the others. I never saw him again that day.

At 11:00, two other people showed up who explained to me that the others had to attend to house repairs—that is, scooping up mud to plaster the sides of the house—and would come soon. What had begun as a small bit of anger and a large amount of frustration on my part slowly subsided, as I remembered Kapuściński's passage. I relaxed. I pulled out my novel and started reading, thinking that I could still give the same lesson, whether at 10:00 a.m., noon, or later that afternoon. After all, what was I there for if not to teach?

And so it was with many of our meetings. I found it a refreshingly human-centred approach, a reminder of why we have meetings in the first place: to gather people together to discuss what needs to be done, what had been accomplished already, what could be improved; a chance to teach and to learn. The conflict occurred, of course, in the need to submit reporting and results consistent with the European view of time, as per NGO and government funding requirements. As another RTP coach put it, "The stress comes because everything takes longer, but you still have the same amount of work to get done."

And while work in the camp itself was always challenging and often trying, my biggest personal challenge came from the intense relationship that I kept up with Caroline, my colleague and roommate. The set-up would have been difficult for anyone, let alone two people so dissimilar. We had known each other for a week before departing and were forced to act essentially as a married couple who both lived and worked together. I realized that as much as I considered myself the type who could get along with nearly anyone, I was also accustomed to having friends who adjusted to the pace at which I got things done.

In the early weeks of our work, the differences had already begun to show themselves. On a few occasions, I would push to spend more time at the camp, while Caroline insisted on heading back as there was nothing more to be done on that day, or we would miss our ride back to Kibuye. I wanted to talk more and learn more, and figured we would find our way back somehow; she was the pragmatist, with our monthly reports clearly in mind, and much less amenable to playing it by ear.

In early June, Caroline cashed in her two weeks of vacation and made her way to Tanzania, while I stayed behind and started feeling to some small extent that the Atlasian weight had been lifted from my shoulders. Finally, I thought, I was left with the freedom to make decisions on the fly, to do things my way. This time apart made me realize that in fact there was a My Way, a way that I worked best, when I was happiest and most efficient. This way, which I found to be typically Rwandan in many respects, involved leaving enough time to observe what was going on in front of me, to chat with people who had something to discuss, to accept offers to sit down and have a drink in someone's house. Leaving room for such human-centred tangents I found to be the only real way to understand the quotidian goings-on of a community, those existing between monthly reports, ID cards, and food distribution.

The realization that each of these approaches—Caroline's and mine—have their time and place, and were in fact complementary, occurred to me only after I had returned home and started my master's degree. Struggling once again with self-imposed and institutional deadlines, I regretted not having someone around to remind me of what had to be done, by when, and why, someone always two steps ahead and planning a full month or more in advance. What struck me most was that the people with whom we work best, whose habits best complement our own, are not necessarily the people we like. Though Caroline and I had both chosen to cross over to *el otro lado*, I found it ironic that I felt more of a connection on many levels with the Congolese and Rwandans I worked with than with a fellow Canadian.

INTROSPECTION

During my many hectic days adjusting to work in the camp and negotiating my relationship with Caroline, my mind would revel in the small bits of solitude and relaxation I found. These moments led me to places where I could meditate on my surroundings, the day's events, and the people I had met.

There was a boat moored on the edge of the lake, for example, that did not move the entire time I spent in Rwanda. It seemed able to seat at least ten for slow, motored tours across the water. Once, while waiting for some friends to come out of a meeting, I walked down to it and got in, pulled out my book, and began to read. The boat lolled, swayed, and rocked me in my reading, moving with the waves and letting an even breeze blow across my neck. I looked up, and the boat's canopy—plastic sheeting, of course—caught the sunlight reflected off the cool, rippling water, interference patterns of light and dark, a constant, random motion, a Brownian ballet.

The trip to the camp itself was for some odd reason another time to clear my thoughts. Friends have mentioned that they often do their best planning while doing something repetitive at the gym. For me, my mind was most focused during the violent side-to-side jouncing of our car, forcing my senses to retreat from the physical world, buffering my nerves and allowing me to plan my day, checking off the things that needed to get done, and, perhaps most important, putting together the theories, ideas, and experiences that led to my epic emails.

Looking out through the car windows, our Land Rover gleaming white on the barren, red dusty paths considered roads, I could not help but note that the term *black*, at least as applied to people, was an unbelievable misnomer. People in Rwanda, as I am sure in many places in Africa, are all shades of brown, from light cappuccino to a darkness, especially on the darkest, sweat-drenched skin, approaching polished ebony. Noses wide and nostrils flared, underlined by bright white teeth and pink gums—made all the more distinct against the darkness of the complexion—and hairless skin often so perfectly smooth that despite knowing how uncomfortable I became when others stared at me, sometimes I could not help but stare.

Being immersed in this richness of skin tones and unfamiliar features, I was sometimes struck by a very vivid sense of my own ugliness. It is not ugliness born of "Oh my God, this dress makes my butt look big; I can't go to the prom looking like this" self-consciousness, thankfully discarded into the rubbish bin of adolescence. It is an aesthetic ugliness. I feel like an eyesore, as if you were to happen upon a McDonald's in the middle of the rain forest, or a blackfly in your chardonnay.

I have been fashioned in an entirely different mould from Rwandans: a long, angular face, offset by a pointed, aquiline schnozz, with the sickly pink or peachy yellow skin that is associated with illness in Africa. I am covered in ever-increasing quantities of hair, and perhaps worst, cannot carry off near-baldness like almost every other man there. I am prone to changing colour in the sun (usually unevenly, given a little time at the beach), or with exercise, or embarrassment, leading to yet another term—*coloured*—that should be redefined and turned on its head.

I found myself knocked nearly speechless at times, lost in the depths and distinctness of the faces I saw: bright-eyed, inquisitive children; *mzes* (old men), whose withered faces had been dragged down and massaged into wrinkles by the tireless sculptor's hands of time; and beautiful, dark cocoa-skinned women, impossible braids planted along their heads like rows of sorghum sprouts. I realized that to be surrounded in such a distinctive otherness meant necessarily to adjust one's own sense of beauty, as if to focus my eyes through the looking-glass of my own perception for the first time onto a new set of features. Characteristics that I once would have described as good-looking about myself now paled (no pun intended) amid the dark, striking, wonderfully varied characteristics of the people I met.

My being singled out as different was not based solely on my appearance but on internal characteristics as well, most notably religion. One day, toward the middle of my six months, I stepped in to one of the many local restaurants dotting Kibuye: small, concrete buildings, usually with only a few tables and chairs and a curtain covering the doorway in lieu of a proper door. Most offer similar fare, with a *mélange* (a heaping plate of rice, beans, starchy plantain, and spaghetti noodles, with a bowl of tomatoey sauce) being the best value, at roughly sixty American cents. For an extra twenty cents, you can have the *mélange avec viande*: your sauce comes with hunk of goat meat in it.

On this particular day, I sat down with some reading material, ordered the requisite *Fanta à l'orange ikonje* (cold orange Fanta), and delved into my book. At a table across from me sat two men and a woman, chattering away in Kinyarwanda. I looked up, and the man in the middle made eye contact. My gaze met his, I smiled, mumbled a hello, and returned to my book. A few minutes later, he approached my table, introduced himself as Gaston, and we realized that we had actually met briefly before. He invited me over to his table. I looked over at large, half-empty beer bottles sitting in front of his friends—it was only noon—and hesitantly accepted. I ordered a Primus, the locally brewed beer, and joined in the conversation as best I could. Luckily they all spoke French, so they asked me where I was from, what I was doing, and how my Kinyarwanda was coming along. Gaston then continued:

"If I may ask, what religion do you follow?"

They seemed like a nice group. I thought I'd give it a shot, and let down my guard. "I'm Jewish."

"Jewish? What's that?"

Admittedly, that was unexpected. I had already met many people in my travels who had never met a Jew before, but total unfamiliarity with the faith was a new one for me. Where to start?

"Well, it's a religion similar to Christianity and Islam [both of which could be found in Kibuye] in that we all share similar stories from the Old Testament."

"What are the basic beliefs of your religion?"

"Well, very basically we believe in the ten commandments—don't kill, honour your parents, et cetera, and what is contained in the Five Books of Moses—but the difference with Christians is that we believe Jesus was a prophet, not the Messiah. We're still waiting for the Messiah."

"So you're Protestant?"

"No, because Protestants are also Christians. We're a different religion completely. You know the people living in Israel right now? Many of them are Jewish, like me."

"Okay, here in town there are churches for Anglicans, Catholics, and Adventists, as well as the mosque. What church do you go to?"

"Well, there isn't any place for me here, because it's a different religion entirely."

"So you're Protestant."

Sigh. "No! There aren't any people from my religion here in Rwanda. In Africa, you find many in the north—Morocco and Algeria—and a bunch in South Africa. There used to be quite a few in Ethiopia, too, but many have left."

"Hunh. Okay, this coming weekend is Easter for us. When do you celebrate Easter?"

Sigh.

Another friend of Gaston's walked in at this point, introduced himself as Léopold, and sat down. The conversation turned to Easter again, and he also inquired about my religious persuasion. He was, unfortunately, little better informed: "Jews? Hunh. I put them in the same line as Hussein and bin Laden. Ce sont des païens...." (They're all pagans....) Major sigh.

I chuckled at the comment—not nervously but because I actually found it funny—and realized how important it was to take these things with a grain of salt. I finished my beer, excused myself, and moseyed home.

The experience with the group at the restaurant made me realize that there are two sides to how I interact with the world. There is the side that I present, over which I retain some amount of control. In this instance, I chose to define myself as Jewish, though I could just as easily have lied and said that I was Protestant, Anglican, or Zoroastrian, in the name of avoiding a confrontation. This self-determination is my identity, the way that I choose to see myself and present myself to others: Canadian, Jewish, book smart, left wing, and so on. I could just as easily lie about any of these, depending on the context. In contrast, and much more insidious, are my intrinsic characteristics, those which affect the way I see the world. I am a man, for example, and thus can never completely understand women (which often goes without saying). I am also Canadian, and Jewish, and Caucasian, and middle class and from Toronto, and all these facets of my upbringing form lenses through which I see the world. The distinction between these two sets of attributes is subtle but noteworthy, in that you can exercise some degree of control over the former, while the best you can hope for is an acknowledgement of the latter. When I write, I realize that I am writing about people whom I cannot, by definition, truly understand, and thus will always be writing from the point of view of a Canadian, Jewish, Caucasian, middle-class, et cetera, et cetera young man. These are my biases, and to acknowledge them is a step toward a better degree of self-understanding and a more honest view of the world.

ANSWERING RAMIRO'S QUESTION

Friends to whom I put Ramiro's question—Why do we do it?—many of them having also ventured into the developing world, answered it in various but related ways. "We are a curious species, and dislike routine," said one. "We're a mixture of idealism, curiosity, and perhaps recklessness, with a good old-fashioned desire to learn about the world so we can make a difference," said another. "All I know is that I love adventure, I love experiencing new things and meeting new people. That is, to me, life in a nutshell," intoned a third. Graced with so much time to reflect on my experiences, I have only to conclude that the reasons we start out with are not the reasons we would necessarily give by the end of our adventures.

The journey to *el otro lado* allows one to cross over many borders: geographical, spiritual, emotional. From a new vantage point, we are given the ability to look back on our regular lives and, by being in a place so alien to our sensibilities, are forced into almost daily introspection. Like my friends, I set out for Rwanda, and indeed all of the other places I have been before and since, with a sense of adventure and restlessness in my heart, a profound curiosity about the world and the people in it, and a sense of idealism that maybe, somehow, I could make a difference. What I gained from these experiences lent me nothing to quell any of these feelings but served only to heighten them. My experiences made me realize that traversing the borders that normally separate me from others has had the effect of collapsing my reactions, limitations, and emotions down to their very base, leaving me to discover things about myself that I did not know, both personally and professionally.

I began to understand that every landscape we see is a product of many forces—human and physical alike. Every mountain, every town, is a congruence of political, social, geophysical, and biological processes, shaping the way that things are today. These things have been changing, at various rates, over history, and will continue to do so. To best understand a place, we should at least have some idea of these forces and how they have interacted over time. This was what drove me to pursue geography as a postgraduate degree.

With respect to my own growth, I learned the extent of my patience, measured my strengths, sighed at my weaknesses, and defined where my comfort zone lies. I learned that there are many ways to see the world, and as we interpret our surroundings we are naïve if we do not first realize and accept our own biases. I learned just how deep culture can run, as even the ways that I view the passing of time or the measurement of beauty are up for debate. I learned, however painfully, that to prosper in the workplace and indeed in the family of my future, I must learn not only to rely on myself and my habits but also to seek out relationships with people whose qualities best complement mine. Finally, and most important, I learned that despite all the differences we are used to seeing aggrandized in an all-too-often biased and alarmist media, we are all human, will laugh at the same jokes, appreciate a well-cooked meal, and ache to communicate by any means at our disposal.

When I return to Mexico with my findings later this year, crossing back over the Rio Grande to an *otro lado* of my own, I fear that I will not have the luxury of these many pages to answer the simple question "Why are you here?" But if I do see Ramiro, and he or his neighbours give me that incredulous glance that has given me so much to think about, there is little that needs to be said.

Para mejor conocer. To better understand.

8

Friendship, Inequality, and Professional Development

Julia Paulson

You often hear from those reflecting on early experiences of development work that what they gained far outweighs what they were able to give. While there have been some publications on the subject, much more has been written in dusty travel journals, detailing the tangible and often shocking ways in which we learn about the world, ourselves, and in the process, our own places in the world. In journals, emails home, and conversations with fellow travellers, development interns question the impact that we, as young people possibly embarking on careers in this area, can have. We question our intentions and find our perspectives of the field and our role in it changing. We take in the sights of jungle landscapes, shanty towns, or island paradises and find ourselves missing "home" just as often as we criticize it and the way it so easily comforts and shelters us. We witness poverty first hand and pause to sit with it, to let the reality of it sink in. At times, we also turn from it, seeking solace in Westernized cafés and hotels, resting in a place of familiarity as we reflect upon new and sometimes disturbing sights, sounds, realities. We also think about the people we are learning from.

Spending time overseas, we begin to craft a life in this new, however temporary, home. We build friendships, struggling, and often laughing, as we work through dynamics distinctly different from those with friends back home. We bridge cultural divides, overcome language barriers, and move across racial and religious differences to find deep companionship and affinity. We grapple with issues of power, privilege, poverty, and opportunity.

What have I learned from these new-found friendships? What have I gained from the people whose position in life and experience of poverty has, in fact, employed me? How do these friendships shape the experiences that eventually become well-turned lines on my CV?

If I could choose my ideal CV format, it would list people chronologically, mapping my personal and professional development by the things the people in my life have taught me, the ways they have shown me how to live. Starting with childhood and curving through my years in school, the names of my parents, teachers, and wise friends would be highlighted. The early pages of this CV, for it would be long, would contain mainly Anglo-Saxon–sounding names because I grew up in a largely white suburb outside Edmonton. Around the year 2000, the names would start to change, with African and Latin American names dominating certain sections as I began to travel. These names would include some of the hardest and some of the simplest lessons learned. Many would be written in capital letters.

Maybe, if I wrote my CV this way, it would not be so dramatically different from those of the friends I write about here. As it is, I have a CV and several of them do not. I have gained valuable skills and professional insights from time spent in the homes and communities where friendships blossomed. I have benefited not only by learning from these opportunities but also because they have led to future opportunities.

When it was time for me to return home, these friends have hugged me goodbye and gone back to their homes and communities with, I imagine, about as much (or, more accurately, as little) opportunity as they had before.

Sometimes, it seems remarkable to me that friendship can exist across such different sets of life experiences. Is friendship able to ignore difference? Does it also submit to the power dynamics and structures that breed inequity? Can it reconcile or bridge them? Or does it simply grow in the cracks, conscious of difference and alternately vocal and strangely silent about it? Maybe friendship is a unique kind of relationship, one that dares to challenge these pretexts, though sometimes getting tangled in them, leaving tear-stained cheeks and exposing deep-set ills. Maybe these are impossible questions, since I will never know exactly how my friends have experienced our relationships. What I can do is reflect on what I have learned and what I have gained compared to what I have given. It is this getting and giving that I ponder the most, wondering if the balance I aim for can actually be achieved. This is what makes the lessons of my relationships with the people I've worked with meaningful and valuable, not just professionally but individually. I like to think that these relationships, while they do not appear on my CV, are in many ways the ones that most qualify me as a professional in a murky field.

FRIENDSHIP: AHMED, DECEMBER 2000–MAY 2001, TAMALE, GHANA

Although he was a couple of years older than I was, twenty-two I think, when I met Ahmed he was still in high school. He didn't go to his classes very often, but he did go by the school almost every day when it let out, to meet with friends and flirt with the girls. He was thin and tall and cute, with beautiful brown eyes and a lovely smile. He had long eyelashes and long hands and he made me feel good when he looked at me. We looked at each other a lot, Ahmed and I. We talked about complicated futures and imagined me behind market stalls and him working at some never clear job, coming home to a dusty house in the evening. We never touched. Ours was a chaste and laden friendship. I think he had a few girlfriends but he would never admit so to me. He was waiting, he said, until he had enough money to take his first wife.

Tamale, where I lived with my Canadian university classmates, is one of northern Ghana's largest cities. It is warm and welcoming, with a colourful market and a lot of orange dust. It is where the Sahel begins its slow dribble into the Sahara. The tropical forests of the South disappear and the terrain flattens, dries, and bakes to a cracked umber. Spooky-looking baobab trees grow fat and tall in isolated beauty and temperatures reach fifty degrees Celsius in the dry season. It is a largely Muslim area, much poorer than southern Ghana, and isolated from much of the country's development. As one travels northward in Ghana the languages spoken, the religions practised, the ethnicities present, and the dominant cultures all change. As in the rest of West Africa, the country was drawn by north–south colonial lines, while ethnic groupings in the region spread from east to west, making for dramatically changing cultures as one travels up from the coast. The landscape follows suit, shifting from tropical and lush landscapes at the sea's edge to the once densely forested capital, Accra, and becoming gradually drier, dustier, sparser until the land reaches the orange of the Sahel in Tamale.

When I was there, Tamale had one main paved street, which cut straight through town. It is one of the few highways connecting north and south and therefore has quite a bit of traffic. Aside from this road, along which the city had expanded vertically, forming a long, narrow band of settlement, most of Tamale's transit ways were rutted mud roads. The city felt very rural as many of its inhabitants lived in mud huts or big, sprawling communal family compounds with plenty of open space between them. Motorcycles and bicycles were the primary means of transport, and everyone and everything seemed to be rambling.

In Ghana, I learned that I can bathe myself and my hair completely with half a bucket of freezing cold water. I went on my first motorcycle ride. I handwashed my clothes in a dusty yard while half a village laughed. I took baby steps into tentative friendships with local girls who called me sister, friendships that turned solid as we began to cook and crochet together. I filled three or four journals' worth of reflections. I was nineteen.

While in Tamale I lived, with four or five of my classmates, in a one-storey cement house with a large front yard. There was a beautiful, lush green mango tree in the yard, and each morning it dropped small, plump mangoes that we would gather to eat for breakfast. I would light a small coal fire in the bottom of the crumbling iron stove we used for cooking, and while fanning the coals and yawning, boil water for our Nescafé early each morning.

I met Ahmed through Yussif, who was the owner of the cement house. Yussif was the head of a very large family, all of whom lived in or around the huge compound neighbouring our house. He worked as a driver at Tamale's largest NGO, where we took our classes. Ahmed was part of Yussif's extended family, as were most of the friends I made while living there. Yussif's compound house was also a single-storey, cement building but much larger and more mazelike than our own, with more decoration and a TV that was permanently playing Rambo videos to a constant collection of spectators. The house opened onto a very large courtyard where all the cooking was done. Other, smaller houses and mud huts in the compound joined the courtyard as well and it was in one of these that Ahmed lived.

Most of the young people who lived on Yussif's compound came over to visit us frequently. Initially we sat around awkwardly in our concrete living room, timidly asking each other questions. Then we began doing crafts. We bought crochet materials in the market and the girls sat with us and showed us crocheting secrets. Through our hours of crochet we became friends, especially with Fatima, a lovely, rambunctious young girl, and with Memenatu, who was near our age and serene. Ahmed would come in and out, bored with our crochet and with the slow, plodding way we worked toward friendship. For him friendship came with a joke. As he had many jokes, he quickly made us his friends. Then, he ignored our delicate and respectful friendship-making with Memenatu and Fatima and the other girls, and burst in on our crocheting hoping to distract us, and hoping we would distract him. We all had plenty of time, living as we were in the heat and the slowness of Tamale, and so we were easily distractible.

Ahmed and I would wander through Tamale, stopping to speak with the different vendors along our paths. They sold fried plantain, delicious fried bean dumplings, a rice and bean dish called red-red, dish detergent, candies, and homemade soap. Ahmed told me little things about the vendors and their families and sometimes pointed out their houses as we passed them. He imagined me into this world by quizzing me about how I would cook red-red, making sure I got the best price for my tomatoes, teaching me the proper greetings to suit the time of day. We would wheel my old-school pastel purple bicycle along with us and take turns riding it. Sometimes I would not see him for days, and sometimes he would fill all my days in a row. He would ask me about Canada and I would try to imagine him into there. He liked to hear about hockey and laughed through my description of the equipment, imagining his narrow face in a helmet. He wondered what he would do there, and I couldn't really imagine it any more than I could imagine myself melting shea butter for red-red day after day. We never told each other that our imaginations could not quite muster what we were asking them to do; we just laughed at the images. I was stunned to find myself daydreaming my way into a world that months ago had existed for me only as a distant television image. For me, Africa had quickly moved from an incomprehensible continent of suffering to a place where I visualized myself in a community, complete with its daily undertakings, dynamics, and nuances, wondering if they could ever become my own.

Ahmed had grown up in a smaller town farther north. He had come alone to Tamale to join his extended family and attend the better high school, which he did very lazily. In his village had been a river, and in it, as a child, he'd learned to swim. It had never occurred to me that hardly anyone in Tamale could swim. Ahmed told me so while boasting about the uniqueness of his swimming prowess and explained that this was why the concrete swimming pool on the outskirts of town was not very well used. I tried to imagine growing up without swimming, but again couldn't. I insisted that we go to this pool right away. We doubled on my bike and peered over the fence at what was indeed a pool though a bit shabby, shallow, and small.

We didn't swim that day, but we went back the next day, after gathering all the neighbourhood bikes so that the children from Yussif's compound could join us. In the pool Ahmed showed off his dazzling aquatics. I lightly held my hands under children's backs telling them to stick their bellies up and relax their heads back so that they would float, just as I'd done with so many children back in Canada, where I'd taught swimming lessons. We splashed and laughed and sunlight sparkled. Children crawled over me and called me sister. I laughed, blew bubbles at them in the water, and finally felt that there was something that I could give them, some way that I could contribute. I could suddenly imagine myself with a life in Tamale, imagining the dusty little town with some of West Africa's best swimmers. Looking across the water at Ahmed, who had facilitated this feeling and given me the pool, I felt I should stay in Tamale forever. In giving me a friendship and a dream, Ahmed had made a place for me; if not entirely comprehensible, at least it was not alien, and I felt emboldened.

With one hand supporting her younger brother, I held the other under the small of Fatima's back, coaxing her to float. I did a handstand for them and they laughed for ages. I swam the length of the pool underwater and became a hero. In Ghana, most of the children who grow up next to the ocean do not learn to swim. Even most of those who grow up on fishing boats do not learn to swim. And certainly those who grow up in Tamale do not learn to swim. Our swimming lessons were my small taste of heaven and their dip into the foreign.

On the way home, Ahmed and I gave up our bike and walked behind the group. "Sister Julie," he said, "I wish you would go to church with the Christians." He went on to explain to me that he was worried about my soul and did not want me to go to hell. I asked him why he thought I should become a Christian and not a Muslim like him. He laughed at me. "White people are Christians," he told me. "Black people are Muslims." I didn't question him, but instead told him that maybe I'd go to church that Sunday, even though I knew I wouldn't. I squeezed the water from my hair into my hands and flicked it at him and felt the truth of that last imagining fade away.

I didn't stay in Tamale forever; I left about a month later. Ahmed kept my pastel purple bike and last I heard, the kids still go to the pool. People ask me if Tamale was very poor and I say yes, but what I remember most about Tamale is laughter. To me, this memory does not diminish the poverty, or the injustice of it, nor assert that in poverty people do not suffer. Rather, it reminds me that people in poverty also laugh—a lesson that seems so straightforward now, but one that I couldn't grasp in my small Canadian suburb. I could only fully grasp it because of Ahmed, because of friendship.

HOMESTAY: DOÑA JULIANA AND FAMILY, APRIL 2003, ESTELÍ, NICARAGUA

In Nicaragua, my friend Paige and I spent a month living in a dusty northern city called Estelí. Estelí was the first city that the leftist Sandinistas took control of in their long fight against the Somoza dictatorship in the 1970s. Now the city is known for its murals, long walls covered in colourful waves swirling out messages about environmental conservation, the rights of women, peace, and respect for the elderly, all painted by local young people and children. These images and messages brighten the church and school and decorate the fences that line the roads of this otherwise unremarkable place. The mural artists were participants in projects led by an NGO called FUNARTE that Paige and I were volunteering with.

Lola, the energetic, inspiring woman who had founded the organization, had set us up to live in her mother's house for the month. Her mother was called Doña Juliana and because she and I were thus nearly *tocayas*—women who have the same name—we had an instant bond. Unfortunately for Paige, while Doña Juliana never forgot my name, she could never remember or pronounce Paige's. Rather than attempting to do so, as the younger members of the household did, Doña Juliana preferred to speak only to me. When she had finished preparing a meal, with Paige sitting nearby, she would call out to me, "Julia, Julia, dinner's ready. Tell your friend."

Doña Juliana had long grey hair that she wore in a bun, and thick, black-rimmed glasses. She wore a skirt that she pulled up just below her breasts and a series of T-shirts with American slogans that she tucked into the skirt so you could just read the first bit. She smoked a perpetual cigarette. She also had a parrot, a lovely new puppy whom she called Necia, which translates as "nuisance," and an older, very anxious, fat dachshund with one surprisingly long incisor that stuck straight up and out of his mouth. Because of this distinctive feature, Paige and I didn't mind that the dachshund had no name; it was obvious to us that he was destined to be called Tooth. Tooth, Necia, and the parrot spent long afternoons sitting on the front veranda of the house with Doña Juliana's very old, very senile, and very deaf husband. He always wore dark aviator glasses, through which his gaze backed you into a corner, while he mumbled and gesticulated in a Spanish that I was never able to understand, no matter how good my language skills got. Despite looking thin, frail, and sinewy, this man was strong and resolved in his madness. His family had learned not to try to restrain him when he got whims to do things such as climb tall trees and camp out at the top for hours.

Doña Juliana and her husband had a large family of grown children. Lola was the only one who still lived in Estelí. There was a daughter in the United States, a son in Canada, a third absent child, and a son who had been killed fighting for the Sandinistas. His painted portrait hung above the kitchen table. The children of Doña Juliana's daughter in the United States were being raised in Estelí, and so we lived with two earnest teenagers whose posters of Britney Spears and the Backstreet Boys fought for primacy with their grandparents' old, yellowing Sandinista FSLN posters.

Most days Doña Juliana served us breakfast, lunch, and dinner. These meals nearly always consisted of rice and beans. Sometimes an egg or fried plantains would adorn them. *Riiiice and beeeans* was worlds different from *rice and beans*, which was different from *riceandbeans*. In other words, sometimes the rice and the beans were served separately, sometimes mixed together, and sometimes mixed with bits of onion and pepper; no matter the arrangement they were always delicious. Rather than dread them for their monotony, as we expected to, Paige and I began to crave them. They were our thrice daily drug and sustained us through the workshops we led at FUNARTE.

At times up to fifty children would turn up for the workshops, eager to make jewellery with the beads and materials we'd gathered through donations in Canada and had trucked around in our backpacks as we made our way down to Nicaragua from Mexico. We would supervise the knotting and tying and weave in the pretty stones the children brought along, dazzled by the way their rambunctious energy could be channelled into a piece of string. At lunch time we walked home from the NGO offices, crossing a nearly dried-up river by stepping on tottering stones. The river used to flow swiftly and had separated neighbourhoods that were also divided by political stance and allegiance in the 1970s. We lived on what had been the Sandinista side of the river, a brave *barrio* still proud of its role in the overthrow of Somoza's harsh dictatorship. The politics of the river now seemed to be more about the environment than about factions; its dwindling current was the subject of a FUNARTE mural painted on International Water Day. We made jewellery with the children and grandchildren of those who had lived through the fighting and watched as the FUNARTE staff worked out sensitive ways to talk about the war and creative ways to express the value of peace. Then we walked home through a maze of murals, a landscape of political meaning, to a meal of rice and beans. To Doña Juliana's kindness and her cigarettes, to posters of Britney Spears. In these *barrios* lived people whose situations we'd heard about in university classes on Latin American politics, in lectures on revolutions, in films about American imperialism. Now, years later, we created jewellery with their children, ate lunch in their sparse kitchens, and nicknamed their pets.

Over a meal at the creaky kitchen table, Doña Juliana gazed at the painting of her son who had been killed in the uprisings. In the painting he wore green fatigues with a red star embroidered on his lapel and carried a rifle. He stared out of the frame bravely. He was young. "When the army came," Doña Juliana said, "I hid under this table with the younger children. Most of the other families in the *barrio* fled, but I wouldn't go. I refused to go. I thought I'd rather die in my home than run."

Paige and I listened to her with dumb nods, never having experienced anything remotely similar yet still moving our heads in something that was supposed to mean understanding and convey empathy. "Did the soldiers come in?" one of us asked.

"Oh yes," replied Doña Juliana. "Oh yes, they came in. But they didn't see us." She stood and began clearing the plates, shooing Necia out of the way.

There were bullet holes left in the front wall of Doña Juliana's home, and her eldest son was only a portrait on a wall. Still she kept the doors to her house open, she kept parrots and puppies and her stove was always warm. In Doña Juliana's house, Paige and I mused and whispered about what "normal" was, what normal could be. How different was normal in this community, in these homes, from the normal in the homes Paige and I had grown up in. Here bullet holes, Western dreams, inspired daughters, lost sons, senility, cigarettes, and humble rice and beans were normal. As we were welcomed into this normal, we also fell into its routines. Routine, Paige pointed out, was never what one thought of when thinking of this place and its politics and its history, and yet here we were waking up as part of one in a household in Estelí. Another lesson, now so clear, then not so: history, an event we analyze from afar, does not stop the place it happens in. It does not freeze the people who live through it. It shapes their normal and adds bullet holes to their façades, but they, too, live past it, as people in Estelí do, by colouring their walls with paint.

COLLEAGUE: JESÚS, SEPTEMBER 2003–DECEMBER 2005, LIMA, PERU

Jesús is a common Spanish name, but having a good friend with this name often made me giggle, especially when sending emails home in which I spoke about "my friend Jesús." Whether he lived up to his name or not, Jesús is one of the kindest, most giving people I have ever known. When I arrived in Peru, excited to begin an internship with Manos Libres, a locally run NGO, I found that they were, at that moment, entirely without funding and therefore without projects. Despite this, Jesús was in the office every day, working on proposals and trying to keep everyone positive. He was always the first to arrive in the mornings, despite the fact that he wasn't being regularly paid. He was there more frequently than my lively bosses, the inventive dream team of Pati and Amparo, who found each other while working in a bank and from each other drew the motivation and the courage to found an NGO and to try to contribute to change in what they called their *Peru querido*, their dear Peru.

Jesús came from one of what we in English call shanty towns, and what Peruvians in Spanish call *pueblos jovenes*, "young towns." These flank Lima on all sides except to the west, where the city stops at the edge of tall mud cliffs that fall into a grey sea. While Peru's interior holds some of the most stunning and picturesque parts of the South American Andes and the Amazon rain forest, this beauty is largely absent from its coastline and its capital city. Lima is in the middle of a desert, impressive only to the degree to which it is indeed a desert. It gets almost no rain and therefore has hardly any green growth outside of the wealthy neighbourhoods, where green can be watered and manicured. Lima spends most of its time fogged in with cold, thick, grey humidity, and when this lifts for the summer it is stifling.

In the centre of this city of nine million are pavement, roads, colonial architecture, and modern buildings that offer a sense of detachment from the surrounding desert. In the *pueblos jovenes*, one does not forget the desert. Here the sand rolls in hilly dunes and the shacks

must be built to cling to this shifting surface. In a more recently established settlement, where the city has yet to provide a reinforced stair-
case, climbing through the steep and sandy town is an arduous task.
Most of the settlements have makeshift schools, some with running
water, some with electricity, both legally and illegally wired. Some of
the settlements are within reasonable distance of a municipal clinic. As
far as I know, none have green spaces, tree shade, or sidewalks to keep
sand from your shoes. Garbage collection is scarce, as are sewage and
drainage systems.

Jesús' family, like so many others, came to Lima from the interior, the *provincias*. They settled, like so many others, in a *pueblo joven*
and diligently pursued the better opportunities that had brought
them there. In many cases, particularly during the 1980s and 1990s,
urban migration was less motivated by the prospects it offered than
by the necessity to flee political violence. At that time, many parts of
Peru suffered and people fled due to the civil war fought between the
Marxist-Maoist group Sendero Luminoso (Shining Path) and government forces. Many victims of this conflict were poor farmers from
the Andean and jungle regions of Peru who were caught between the
fighting forces, both of which presumed them guilty. For government
forces, these peasants were Sendero Luminoso terrorists, while for
Sendero fighters they were complicit with the government and against
their revolution. The 2003 Truth and Reconciliation Commission of
Peru estimates that the majority of the over sixty-nine thousand people
who were killed during this period came from indigenous communities and were not involved in fighting on either side.

After their move to Lima, Jesús' mother raised him and his siblings alone, working odd jobs and becoming an involved community
leader. She had been taught by her grandmother to read coca leaves
and came to our office one day to read mine, Pati's, and Amparo's. We
crowded around a desk as Jesús' mother chewed up the bundles of
dried leaves that we had each held in our hands, each blown upon, and
each told our secret wishes to. She mixed the leaves in her mouth with
a chalky white powder that reacts with the leaves to turn them black

and intensify their appetite-suppressing, energy-giving properties. It also slowly rots out the teeth of frequent coca leaf chewers, leaving a black and broken smile. Jesús' mother spat dark saliva onto a sheet of white paper three times, once with each of our leaves in her mouth. She spent a considerable amount of time examining the patterns made, tilting her head from side to side, mumbling "Hmmm, *si, si*" and looking at the one who had blown on that particular set of leaves. She didn't tell us what our spit patterns meant to her. Instead, she put each of the patterns before her and dealt out tarot cards. She told us about futures that did not please any of us. We spent the rest of the afternoon convincing ourselves from across our desks that we didn't believe in coca leaves, or tarot cards, or fortune telling in general. Jesús took his mother home, a journey that involved several different shaky buses and took at least two hours.

The next day he laughed at us and said, "It only matters if you believe in it." For Jesús, belief was supremely important. He didn't mind what it was that you believed, but he felt it was essential that you believed firmly and with conviction in something, some set of personal truths, and that you based your life on those beliefs. He was strongly Catholic, and his belief, mixed with the deep sense of community activism and justice that he had inherited from his mother—which ran through him in a way you felt you could almost touch—shaped his life. He asked me what I believed on the first day I met him, and over our months of lunches together and bus rides into the provinces for work when we finally got a small amount of funding, he slowly drew out of me a sort of manifesto of beliefs that I'd never before seen as a coherent whole. "Don't tell me what you don't believe in," Jesús would always tell me as I tried to deflect his questions. "Tell me what you do believe in."

He called me *querida*, dear, and *pequeña*, small one, and caught me when I fainted at high altitudes. He teased me like my brother does. He was a sort of brother away from home. Despite my problems with his language, he learned to read my tone of voice over the phone. He became the first person I would call, whether I was crying or laughing.

He convinced me that I should learn to cook and praised all of my attempts until they finally became tasty and then told me, "See, I knew you were a good cook," and dropped his praise.

Jesús' work, all of which was severely underpaid, was with and for children. Jesús instinctively knew what a growing body of development literature and NGO research is now telling us, that thinking about development without thinking about it in terms of children is not likely to get us anywhere. He believed in participation and leadership, and resilience among children. He was an inspired facilitator and support for them. When I arrived at Manos Libres, he was trying to develop a youth leadership and human rights project in an Andean city called Puquío. The funding proposal was going to be submitted to the Canadian International Development Agency (CIDA). I told him I could help him with the development, since I was familiar with CIDA's project formats and because I spoke English.

"Great," he said, "but not until you meet the kids in Puquío."

We went to Puquío together, wrote the project together, met with CIDA together, and we should have worked on the project together. During the time we spent developing the Puquío project, my CIDA stipend was the only salary being paid at Manos Libres. Unpaid salaries were not uncommon in the world of Peruvian NGOs, particularly small and new ones like Manos Libres, which depended on funding on a per project basis. Jesús' whole career was a dichotomy of either unpaid salaries—projects that he'd dreamed up and worked on and put his heart into and received little compensation for—or jobs that he'd had to take because he was broke. By the time our Puquío project was finally approved by CIDA, Jesús had had to leave Manos Libres for another job that didn't thrill him but that did pay. We both cried about the timing, but I cried harder. Jesús was used to it.

His absence meant that I had to facilitate a leadership and human rights education project for children that had been designed by and for a master facilitator. Jesús met me in the evenings, coming straight from his new job, to coach me. I searched the internet for games and activities and he laughed at me and told me about ones that he had invented. He brought me to every project he knew of around Lima so that I could meet their facilitators and see how they worked. I got more and more nervous as I made phone calls and sent letters to Puquío, arranging for the first workshop.

Before leaving for the first workshop, I met with Jesús in a panic. "I'm not Peruvian," I told him. "I don't know about their context, I don't speak perfect Spanish, I'm not an educator, I don't even really know very much about human rights, and who says they want to learn about human rights? Who am I to lead a workshop?"

He laughed. "I think they'll be able to tell you aren't Peruvian," he said. He told me that I should do what I knew how to do, and that I might judge what the project was giving the children by what I got from them. When I think about the idea of balance in development work, I see Jesús and myself on our bus ride home from my first trip to Puquío, sleepy and remembering different children's drawings. When I think about inspiration in development work I think about Jesús riding through Lima on a crowded bus with his mother, watching the city, dreaming it differently in his mind.

On that day, the day before I was to leave for my first workshop, I thought about what "I knew how to do." I thought about myself as a child, about what I had liked doing best, about how I had learned best. I went to the hardware store and bought some paint. At my workshops, we played games of the Jesús variety and talked about human rights in my weak attempt at the Jesús way, but the activities that I thought were most effective were the ones for which I gave children paint brushes and a theme. This is very likely because painting is what I knew and loved; it was what I was excited to share.

Five of the children who attended the workshops were elected to come to Lima for a national youth conference. When Jesús came to meet us in Lima, I felt like a proud mama hen introducing them to my tutor. He laughed with them and quizzed them about what they had learned, what they had done in their workshops, what it was like to hang out with a Canadian. He carried them on his shoulders, told them about things he had learned from me, made me blush. The kids stared up at glass buildings, squished into their first elevator rides, holding their breath, and ran along Lima's grey beaches and splashed ocean water at each other. In this week of firsts, Jesús' pride in me made me feel qualified in a way I'd never felt before.

I always find it difficult when preparing a CV to distil my work experience into a few lines that highlight skills and qualifications. Trying to perform such an exercise on a friendship is harder still. We learn from our friends by admiring them, by dipping into their worlds, imagining ourselves into their realities, and then admiring them more still for the ways in which they live and the challenges that they face. In friendships that include wide inequalities, this sense of admiration can be almost overwhelming. At times I felt frustrated, almost crippled, by the gaps between our realities.

What these relationships showed me is that the frustration can be powerful. It can be a tool for small, startling changes. It can bring kids to the ocean for the first time. It is the crippling part of perceived difference—of focusing only on difference—that must be overcome. In these friendships, through laughter, tears, bike rides, phone calls, dreams, and shared meals, it was overcome. Jesús, Doña Juliana, and Ahmed all showed me, often by laughing at me, that to despair over their situations, over their realities, was not helpful. It couldn't change anything. More appropriate, and more empowering, was to be there for the small changes that they were creating and to look for ways to support those. People like Ahmed, Doña Juliana, and Jesús are in all the lines of my CV, shimmering under adjectives like flexible, creative, and motivated. They have informed my career path and my goals, and they have shown me to think that development should be about figuring out ways to make their small changes bigger.

9

Coming Home to Foreignness

Valerie Stam

I was very curious to see how I would feel about being back in Senegal after an absence of a year and a half when it had previously been my home for two. The plane ride was long and sleep depriving. I arrived in Dakar at 8:00 p.m. The sky was deep set in inky blue tones and I could barely discern the outlines of the palm trees that once were so familiar to me. I shrugged off my long-sleeved sweater and inhaled deeply.

I have heard that the first thing to strike you when you step off a plane in Africa is the smell. I am not sure if this is true, but the smell of burning garbage has since become oh so familiar. When I stepped off a Cameroon Airlines aircraft into the Douala airport for my first trip to an African country as a very young fifteen-year-old, it was overpowering. I cranked open my jet-lagged eyelids to visually and mentally adjust to the sea of garbage outside the window slats and the kids scrounging around in it to eke out their existence. Strangely enough, this smell has become a hallmark of my time in Africa, popping up at times in the most unexpected places and infusing me with a sense of homecoming and self. These two feelings are obviously dichotomous: my sense of self was reinforced and created by the fact that I did not belong in Africa; yet I feel a sense of place, a familiarity, with this continent that has played a part in shaping me into who I am. Like a plane touching down and taking off again, the times I spent in Cameroon, Ghana, and Senegal come together in a journey of introspection and reflection on privilege, self, and home.

As a foreigner, I am very aware of myself in West Africa. Unavoidable when one is white in a sea of black faces. Sitting in the back of a decrepit Dakar taxi winding through traffic and around potholes filled with water, I find myself unconsciously scanning faces on the street, looking for other white-skinned people. If and when we do make eye contact, it is generally to square our shoulders and pretend we did not actually see each other. I wonder where this streetwise independence comes from.

Coming from a country where I belong to the majority and growing up in a community known for its ethnic homogeneity, it is disconcerting, to say the least, to find myself a visible minority. I am constantly tense due to the unrelenting stares. Even worse, I am annoyed when people stop to stare fixedly, do a double take, or turn in their seats to get a better view. Perhaps, with our strongly cultivated sense of individualism, as a Canadian I feel frustrated when my actions are deemed representative of all white people. Perhaps I feel uncomfortable being lumped in with the burdensome history and current media stereotypes associated with whiteness. I am only superficially cognizant of my racial baggage since I have the luxury, inherent in positions of power, of choosing when to engage with it rather than being forced to confront it every day. While this experience as a visible minority may help me to relate to minorities in Canada, I doubt I can fully capture their experience in my own. Whiteness, however minor, still holds a privileged position. My actions, couched as they are in an unjust system of class and power, still smack of oppression.

Africa started to interest me when I was about eleven years old. I'm not sure what about Africa I found so attractive at that age. Perhaps I was rebelling against my insular Dutch immigrant community, where home, church, and school all had the same, monotonous look. In my mind, black was as different as one could get. On the other hand, it could be explained simply as curiosity and love of a challenge. My parents often bring up an observation my kindergarten teacher made: "Your daughter will always need something new to interest her." I doubt Mrs. Kloet had the slightest notion that her words would be remembered years down the road, but they have proven true. Sometimes they seem like a curse echoing down the corridor of years, as lack of stimulation sometimes turns to boredom with work, school, and even people. On the other hand, it is what has propelled me into development work and taken me travelling.

At fifteen, I happened to pick up a brochure in my high school guidance office advertising mission trips for teens to southern countries. I immediately seized upon it and scoured its pictures, getting increasingly excited with the turn of each page. Cameroon was described as a mountainous, lush country where pygmies lived and one could buy masks in the marketplace. I am amazed at how such a simplistic and romanticized description tempted fate.

Our mission consisted of dramatizing the story of Christ. After performing this drama on various streets in the city of Douala as many as five times a day, we would go into the crowd that had formed and converse with people, asking them if they had enjoyed the performance and understood the message. Responses were varied, from wildly joyous to downright negative.

One encounter stuck like a thorn in my side.

One of my teammates was conversing with a group of young men. Some of them had questions about the drama, but most were more interested in where we came from and what we were doing in Cameroon. On realizing that our mission was solely to evangelize, one young man became furious. "You come from the richest countries in the world!" he spat out angrily. "How can you come here and talk about God when people are starving and poor?"

While my teammate seemed to shrug it off, the remark entered me like a sliver and embedded itself deeply in my consciousness. The process of digging it out has led to years of reflection and drastically directed my future.

Prior to this conversation, I had been struck by the poverty I was witnessing in Cameroon. Two old trucks carted all fifty of us piled in the back from drama site to drama site. In one, wooden slats formed the frame of the truck bed. This gave ample opportunity to observe the passing scenery. While it was lush and green, with an oppressive humidity, it also appeared extremely poor and mismanaged. There were potholes everywhere, and due to the lack of public toilets, men and women squatted on the side of the street. The sewage system was often exposed, leaving us with the fear of accidentally falling in. Houses appeared to be slapped together with planks of wood, and electricity was sporadic at best. This poverty disturbed my young mind with effects that I could not yet begin to comprehend.

On returning to Canada, I sank into depression. Not only had I encountered a Pentecostal spirituality hitherto unknown to me (which then sent me on a quest for a faith in which I could feel more like myself) but I also mulled over the young man's anger and frustration and the deeper questions of poverty and riches, "us" and "them," and ultimately, justice. These subjects danced in and out of my head and occupied enormous amounts of my time and energy. Unfortunately, being a moody teenager, I also felt them wreak havoc with my emotions.

While these questions have not been entirely resolved (nor do I think they can be), my struggle to answer them has taken me on a journey. On pulling out the thorn in my side and examining it, I discovered that indeed, the young man had been justly frustrated about the state of the world and our (apparent) inaction, given our position of privilege. Moreover, my limited experience with the Church had thus far suggested that it fell short in acting out concern for the poor and against injustice. Preoccupation with the soul meant that the body was neglected. These two epiphanies fused into one and formed the basis for a solid idealism that led me into the world of development, with a grounding in faith and an emphasis on social justice.

DEGREES OF POVERTY AND PRIVILEGE

Yesterday, I dropped off my application for Dutch citizenship.

I also found an ad in my inbox for a comedy show entitled "They're Deporting Him Anyway." A stand-up comedian from Malawi who studied at McGill at the same time I did is being forced to leave the country.

I feel somewhat guilty. Not that I am directly responsible for this man's fate, but once again, I am confronted with my privilege. I am a white woman. I have dual citizenship. Not much has stood in the way of attaining my goals.

Nearing the end of my second year of university, I was so gripped with the desire to make a difference in the world that I seriously contemplated putting my studies on hold. Academia felt lifeless and insular. Fortunately, one stimulating aspect of university life held true: community. I lived in a first-floor apartment with three wonderful women. Musings on academics, our future, boys, and the state of the world permeated the air in our kitchen and on our morning walks to class. One afternoon, while waiting to see my program adviser, I came across a flyer for a study-abroad program in Ghana. I immediately dismissed the exhilarating thought as impossible, mostly because it seemed entirely out of the realm of normal, and settled in for the (inevitably) long wait to see my adviser. Suddenly, one of my roommates, Natasha, rounded the corner. An unexpected place to see her, I thought, as she was a biology major. But she, too, was thinking through her life and contemplating a switch out of biology and into the social sciences.

She took one look at the flyer for the Ghana program I pointed out and said with authority, "You should do it!"

All the way home, I thought through her pronouncement, and "You should do it" became "I *will* do it." Little did I know how much this decision would affect my life.

I grew up in the countryside, first on a pig farm that nearly bankrupted my father, then in a country house big enough to contain my family of seven. We never had a lot of money. We went out for dinner so rarely that I can remember all of the restaurants we ate in. At restaurants, we always ordered water instead of drinks. I remember shopping at Amity before second-hand clothing was cool.

Now I live in a neighbourhood where parents take their preschoolers out for coffee.

Living in Ghana was like plunging head first into icy cold water. At first it paralyzed me. The last time I had been in Africa was five years before and it had been a short-term trip with a large group of culturally and racially similar people. Now I faced Africa as an individual. No longer able to hide behind a group of fifty white teenagers, I attract attention like spilled spaghetti sauce on a white blouse. I had to adjust to speaking Twi in order to take the right *tro-tro* to campus in Accra. Grocery shopping in the chaotic and colourful marketplace often required more courage and gregariousness than I could muster. Being older and less insulated from the people around me also made me more aware of cultural propriety. I agonized over offending people with my cultural insensitivities.

On our return from a five-day baseline assessment in a village in northern Ghana, my classmates and I discussed the poverty we were faced with every day in the country. In the village, I had noticed some children with bloated bellies and orange hair, effects of malnutrition. I wanted to identify with the poverty and the poor people we were in contact with. To my mind, this poverty was similar to poverty experienced in Canada. Maria, a classmate from Mexico, took offence at this comment.

"Given that the poor in Canada have access to social services, they are not really poor," Maria stated categorically.

"We have poor people in Canada! Just because social services exist doesn't mean that everyone is physically or mentally capable of

accessing them. Nor does it mean that it reaches everyone it should."
Having volunteered in a street youth drop-in centre in Hamilton, I
had seen that services going to people living on the street were poorly
funded and an inefficient way to get to the root causes of poverty in
Canada. Yet there was a niggling "but" that wouldn't go away. Maria's
comment made me realize that by trying too hard to identify with
the poor, I might be deriding them, downplaying their suffering. I
wanted equality, even in suffering. But suffering does not come in
equal doses.

LONELINESS

The last four months of the school year in Ghana were spent in a field
placement on a development project with an NGO. Being interested
in conflict zones, I chose to go to a refugee camp housing people from
Sierra Leone, Liberia, and Togo.

Once in the camp, I discovered that the income-generation projects that I had come to work on were no longer functioning, so my
"internship" became a research project. Mr. King, who organized all
the micro-credit and income-generation projects, was my mentor. He
did his best to convince me that I would be happier staying in the tiny
village of Ekwe, about a forty-five-minute walk from the camp. I almost
believed him; after all, the housing was much nicer and it was right on
the Atlantic Ocean. However, staying in the refugee camp turned out
to be the best, and also the hardest, decision of my life.

I was shown to a small, concrete room that already housed two
women, Kadiatu and Mariatu. They had graciously allowed Mr. King
to extend their offer of hospitality to me, an idealistic young Canadian.
The three of us shared a king-sized bed, as well as an open-air bathroom enclosed with bamboo, off to the side of the room. This was
where I took my bucket showers and (in a different bucket) performed
other daily needs. Kadi would later empty the bucket into the latrines,
which under no circumstances was I allowed to use. According to her,
even being near the latrines would result in instant sickness.

My favourite time to shower was in the evening. The water was warm from sitting under the sun all day, offering enough contrast to the cool night air to make me feel cozy. On a clear night, the stars were legion and I could hear the sound of the ocean waves booming in the distance. The crickets would be chirping and everyone would be getting ready for bed, making the soft nighttime people noises common around the world. It felt like being tucked in.

I don't believe times are memorable. Rather, the people whom time finds us with make a particular occasion, or country, as the case may be, stick in one's memory box. The Krisan-Sanzule refugee camp remains a happy place in my mind. Though it was difficult, I felt I grew by leaps and bounds during this time. By contrast, it was like a prison for the refugees housed there.

Kadiatu and Mariatu knew many people in the camp and I was soon introduced to a variety of friends, most of them from Sierra Leone. At the front of our room was a shuttered window facing the road, shaded by a comforting, leafy neem tree. Some of the more ambitious young men of the community had built bamboo benches and a table around this tree and it had become a gathering place for friends and relatives. I spent many happy days watching the rhythms and patterns of refugee camp life and building friendships from under the breezy, shaded canopy of this tree. In the mornings, a convoy of women and children swinging brightly coloured plastic buckets passed beside our room on their way to the water pump directly behind. They returned swaying with full buckets on their heads. Twice a day children dressed in brown and orange school uniforms walked by, some with oversized and underfilled backpacks flopping listlessly in time to their steps. I felt accepted by the community—probably because I shared some of the sufferings of camp life with them, namely poor sanitation and little food. Over time, I became a familiar face and many people started greeting me using my new Sierra Leonean name, Mary. "Auntie Mary! Morning-oh! How dee bodee?" was the familiar Krio refrain. I was blissfully happy in the refugee camp, an emotion that disturbed me as all the refugees were dismally unhappy with their situation of being neither here nor there. I was in my element, learning languages, making friends. For me, the refugee camp was a mini-paradise on earth.... The sun was radiant year round, pineapples grew wild in the forest, and the ocean was just a short distance away. For everyone else, the refugee camp meant poverty, trauma, dislocation, and ambiguity. My friends were scarred, hungry, and debilitated by despair. I had the power to leave when I chose; my friends had little choice but to wait for their situation to change. Though it was always in front of me, never before had I noticed how choice is a defining element of power and privilege. I had never thought of poverty and oppression in terms of withholding choice.

Despite the connection I felt with people, at times I was intensely lonely. No one understood what my culture was like, or why I talked, ate, laughed, and thought the way that I did. Even though I was lonely, I did not want to leave. Rather, I wanted desperately to share my thoughts and emotions with someone who understood me. I wanted a link between my previous world and my current one.

Most of the friends I made are now resettled to the United States or Canada, and we are still in touch to this day. Yet now the tables have turned; it is they who are calling me out of loneliness, trying to make sense out of this new world they live in, and to build the links between past and future. I think, for them, I am such a connection. While I was in Ghana, Ishmael, a Sierra Leonean, constantly plied me with questions about the United States. His family and that of his girlfriend and his friends had successfully applied for resettlement there. "So, Valerie," he drawled one day, "when I step off the plane in America, someone will be waiting there with a job for me, right?" I did my best to burst their media-fed impressions of life in North America, but defeat often silenced me. It was obvious they did not believe me. When I casually mentioned that there were homeless white people in North America, Ishmael's face expressed utter disbelief and astonishment. "How can white people be poor? No, it's not possible!" To this day, I wonder what his reaction was when he did finally see the face of homelessness and poverty in the United States.

Now settled there for five years, Ishmael calls me occasionally. He and his girlfriend have two children. They pay more in rent than they can make in a month. Ishmael dreams of going to school, getting a degree, and even working up to a Ph.D. "I want to be like you when I grow up," he said recently. A disturbing statement. I now have my M.A.; he has just enrolled for his first year of a B.A. We are the same age, yet starting from two completely different levels, principally because of the fate of birth and the colour of our skin.

HOMECOMING AND INTERCONNECTEDNESS

After I completed my B.A., I got a job working in Senegal in peacebuilding and disarmament with a local NGO. While I was crossing over the Atlantic at night on my way to the two-year assignment, the *Joola*, a passenger boat travelling from Ziguinchor to Dakar, sank in the ocean, killing over eighteen hundred people.

As I emerged from my jet-lagged sleep that morning and first set foot in the energetic city of Dakar, I had the bizarre feeling that something had gone terribly wrong. From my previous travels in West Africa, I knew that tears were not an everyday appearance on street corners. But in Dakar grown women sat on the sidewalk crying uncontrollably. People were lined up outside the port authority's office, nervously awaiting news. As was true for most Senegalese, the enormity of what had happened did not quite hit me until many days later, when the government finally released realistic figures. Not normally a superstitious person, I was surprised to find myself thinking that the coincidence of this huge accident and my arrival was a bad omen for the year to come.

I tend to be forward-looking, always placing myself in the future, wondering and planning what comes next, wondering if where I am is where I am supposed to be. I fought against this tendency throughout my two-year stay in Senegal, trying instead to be content with where I was at the moment. It was not easy. However, whenever I was in Ziguinchor, the capital city of the southern region of Casamance, I had a sense of rightness.

One time this contentment arrived as I was driving around town in a blue Jeep with a colleague's child bouncing on my lap. I looked around me and thought, I am perfectly happy right now. A sense of affirmation. A homecoming? All I know is that at that particular moment, it seemed I was seeing myself as I truly felt. I was fully present and living the moment.

It also felt right that one year after my arrival in Senegal I was back in Ziguinchor to commemorate my anniversary, and that of the shipwreck.

I had come to Ziguinchor to attend a forum organized by a women's peace association that lobbies for an end to the ongoing separatist conflict in the Casamance region. The association Kabonketoor (meaning *to reconcile* in Jola) is also deeply spiritual. Preceding the forum and the anniversary of the *Joola* shipwreck, some women performed ceremonies throughout the night in the tradition of their ancestors. The next day, services of prayer and remembrance were held at mosques and cathedrals around town.

Later that day, we followed the president's convoy from the local airport to a cemetery filled with unmarked graves. Many bodies were not recovered from the shipwreck, and those that were had been largely unrecognizable. I found myself in a crowd of people who were crying and praying silently. Once again the enormity of the situation hit me. A colleague had lost his wife and all his children when the boat sank. Now he found himself alone. Casamance, a region already suffering from a separatist conflict for the past twenty years, lost a whole generation of its best and brightest youth, who had been on their way to Dakar for the new school year. Despite my foreignness, I found myself fighting back tears. I had been unreservedly welcomed and made to feel at home by the very people who were facing an enormous tragedy. As the spokesperson for the families of the victims said, "In spite of the tragedy, we can be thankful for the year God has given us." *Santa Yalla. Amin. Amin.* (Thanks be to God. Amen. Amen.)

In the afternoon, at the opening ceremony for the forum, a young Catholic nun got up to speak, having spent the morning praying for the victims of the *Joola* at the cemetery. Not knowing that there was a forum going on, she had found herself led to the conference grounds and in tears interrupted the governor's opening speech. Everyone sensed a spiritual presence speaking through her; there was hardly a dry eye in the room. When the nun had finished, a respected Muslim leader got up to speak. Not understanding Arabic or Wolof, I was still impressed with the commanding presence of this dreadlocked imam swathed in yards of white fabric. His eyes pierced right through me. At the end of his speech, the imam asked us to turn to each other, shake hands, and ask, "Baal ma ak" (Forgive me for everything). A poignant start to a peace conference organized by a group whose name means "reconciliation."

As a Protestant Christian (something very rare in Senegal), I was amazed by the presence of God in this room full of women from the traditional sacred forest associations, Muslims, Catholics, and Protestants. As in other countries in Africa, the lines between religions are very fuzzy here. People easily recognize that God moves in others' experiences, not solely through their own religion. It was moving for me to witness God in such an ecumenical context. I felt I was in the right place at the right time, that there was a reason I was in Ziguinchor at that particular moment, that there was something I needed to see. I finally felt able to answer some of the questions that began in Cameroon when I was fifteen.

Likewise, when I returned to Senegal a year and a half later for a few brief months of field research, I had a brief sensation of homecoming. I felt self-confident in returning to a place that I knew well and that had a loving, affirming community. My old apartment in Dakar was located next to a park housing a giant obelisk, the Monument of Independence. The obelisk was always clearly visible from the plane as it circled the airport to land. While I was living in Dakar during my two-year development contract and frequently flying to other countries in West Africa, seeing the obelisk on the way back always brought a sense of homecoming. When it appeared below me this last time, I felt nostalgic. That was my first apartment—the first place that

I found, furnished, and called home all by myself. I felt the familiar anticipation and then the sharp realization that I would not be going back, that my apartment, my life there, was just a memory.

When returning to Canada, I always feel cut off from whatever reality I have experienced elsewhere. I am less stimulated. The side of me that gets energy from living in a different language and culture and making friends through it all feels dull, like a deadened branch on a still-living tree. For a while, I have one foot planted firmly on either side of the ocean. Later, it becomes an act of willpower for me to envision life as it continues far away for my friends Kadi, Ishmael, and Maria, in different worlds operating synchronically.

Time is strange. I have heard it said that humans are meant to be timeless, that we are hardwired for eternity. Perhaps that is why moving through time zones takes such a toll on our bodies. Perhaps that is why I cannot easily make the mental jump to daily life across the ocean as I sit in a franchised coffee shop in Canada, with computers whirring and kids scraping stools back and forth across the tiled floor, drinking tea that comes handpicked from India.

I believe that the separation that distances and insulates Canadian life from life in poorer countries is manufactured. It is so easy to think in terms of "us" and "them." *The civilized and the savages. Modernity and tribalism.* When we think of the modern world, we think of high-rises, concrete, the high-tech industry, and big box stores. However, my travels have taught me that to be truly honest about the world is to recognize that modernity is an overcrowded and malfunctioning boat shipwrecked in Senegal alongside the gleaming high-rises of downtown Toronto. It is the children with bloated bellies playing soccer in northern Ghana alongside the string of fast-food joints dotting Canadian highways. It is the war of Sierra Leone, with hacked-off limbs and drugged child soldiers, next to entitled, joyriding, university students. Our existence is mutually dependent. Our so-called modern lives would not exist if it were not for the massive slave trade, sweatshops, unequal trade relations, child labour, unfair agricultural subsidies—the list could go on. Our way of life depends on their poverty. If

I think of the world as a whole instead of compartmentalizing regions, countries, and people, I cannot think of modernization in the same way. Modernization has transformed telecommunication to such an extent that I can speak to and see a friend in Japan in real time. Modernization has also compounded massive worldwide inequality.

As I write this, I am in a local fair-trade coffee shop. A father and daughter take the table next to me. She's a little Asian girl, around four years old, and he's a middle-aged white man. She is showing off her clothing in its varying shades of pink and is very affectionate with her father, clambering all over him, demanding a story. He acquiesces, and she snuggles down into his lap, preparing for the childlike bliss of being transported into another time and world.

Almost against my desire, I lean closer (while trying not to appear as though I'm eavesdropping). As I get caught up in the story, my highlighter drops to the floor, snapping me back to attention.

I am reminded of a return trip I made to Cameroon for Christmas a few years ago. While visiting my friend Joseph, with whom I had kept in touch since my first visit, I had the pleasure of staying with his extended family; his wife, seven brothers, sister, mother and father, cousins, and neighbourhood children filled the yard and house with constant activity. One day, I was shelling peas with the other women of the household. We were seated in a circle around a large steel bowl into which we tossed the peas. I was enjoying the female fellowship, which I felt despite language, age, and cultural barriers. I did not say much and, aside from receiving the occasional instruction, I let the laughter and chit-chat wash over me. But as I was shelling the peas, whose pods looked identical, I noticed that they came out in different colours: red, white, and brown. Though I have a basic knowledge of garden produce, this seemed strange. Was it genetic? Perhaps they came from different plants? Maybe the sun discoloured them? Silence descended on the circle after I posed my question. Had I said something really stupid? Her grey-white hair pulled back into frizzy corn-rows, Joseph's grandmother straightened her back, looked me directly in the eye, and explained.

"You see how people are different colours. Clarence, Joseph's sister, is black. You are white. And Valérie, Joseph's wife, is more reddish. In the same way, the peas are different colours."

Satisfied, she went back to shelling the peas. The other women followed her example. I am afraid I had a bemused smile on my face. It was not quite the answer I was looking for, coming from a rational, scientific education system. However, on reflection, I realize that Joseph's grandmother's answer was appropriate to the situation. Here we were, all women, united in our task but coming from entirely different backgrounds. Her allegory taught me lessons of diversity, acceptance, and coexistence as no scientific reasoning could.

Back at the café, I relax into the bench. I appreciate Joseph's grandmother for answering my question in the way she knew best. She, and this father with his daughter snuggled so securely in his lap, demonstrate the parallels between "developed" and "undeveloped," "modern" and "primitive." Story telling, remembering and passing on history, customs, and traditions, is a humble affirmation that we all belong to humanity and, in our desire to pass something of ourselves along, share clumsy aspirations of timelessness. For a moment, instead of fighting to bridge the constructed divide between self and other, us and them, I see it for what it is.

10

You Go and Come

Heidi Braun

Not exactly a typical Friday night out on the town in Nairobi for a visitor. While the *Lonely Planet* might recommend that the tourist sample *nyama choma* (grilled meat) at the Carnivore restaurant, drink Tusker beer, and dance the night away at a sweaty nightclub, I have elected to spend my Friday evening as the only visible foreigner at the downtown bus terminal.

Back in Kenya after almost three years, it seems fitting to return to this old haunt. I spent hours of my past visits here at the Nairobi Akamba station, waiting in line to buy a ticket, waiting longer for a delayed bus. I also suffered hours as a passenger on Akamba buses, making the long trek westward from Nairobi past Kisumu to Ugunja, or heading back from Ugunja to Nairobi.

I first became oriented to Akamba travel while working as a Canadian Crossroads volunteer at the Ugunja

Community Resource Centre (UCRC), a local NGO that worked to improve farming, health, and education for the population in the nearby villages. A seat on Akamba was luxury compared to riding cross-country in an overstuffed mini-bus; the yellow coach buses were markedly more comfortable and safe than the *matatus*. I then logged serious overtime aboard Akamba buses when I came back a year later to do my M.A. research in western Kenya. And now, returning on this third visit to Kenya, it strikes me that the Akamba station is probably one of the most familiar locales in Nairobi to me.

After paying the taxi driver, I step out into the crowd and move toward the familiar yellow paint on the concrete exterior of the station, still a bright beacon for travellers down this otherwise shady street. Darkness has fallen, so I briskly move into the terminal to wait for my friends behind the security of the station walls. The tension in the Nairobi evening air is palpable. Many Kenyans make a point of avoiding nighttime movement in the city centre if possible, and foreigners are emphatically warned against walking even one block once the sun goes down, for fear of being mugged or worse.

I look out from behind the grated station windows. Exhaust coughs from the tailpipe of the bus parked out front and I shift impatiently from left foot to right while I observe the chaotic dance of passengers negotiating heavy loads, weaving through the clogged throngs and alleys near the station off ever-bustling Tom Mboya Street. Despite longing to reconnect with my friends back in Ugunja, I have resolved to spare my body the Akamba travel experience of at least seven hours of disintegrating, pothole-ridden roads during this short visit. I don't have enough time to justify making the long journey west. Nonetheless, my desire to catch up with a few old friends means putting in my time at the Akamba depot, since the only chance to see Rachel, one of my dear colleagues from the UCRC, is to meet before she boards the bus to Ugunja. And the best time to connect with another UCRC colleague, Charles, is when he comes to the city centre to see Rachel safely onto the said bus.

Waiting anxiously for Charles and Rachel to arrive at the station, I tell myself I will be fine. I note how Akamba seems to have cornered gatekeeper status between me and the people and place of western Kenya. The station, a place of waiting, ever the reminder of the value and importance of patience when dealing with things beyond my immediate control. I scan the busy street for Charles. How to distinguish him—a thin black Kenyan man—out of a mob of the same?

After a long few minutes, Charles climbs out of a car and spots me instantly. We shake hands and exchange an awkward hug, happy to see each other after so long. Then we spot Rachel and her family entourage. Their taxi driver is eager to escape the bedlam in front of the station so we help unload and shuttle suitcase after suitcase from the trunk to the back alley where we join the queue with Rachel. The terminal is an unlikely spot for a social gathering, but we do our best with only a few short hours to catch up after years of separation.

I ask about our mutual friend Rose and her family, whom I am most disappointed that I won't be able to visit. We laugh about Rose's habit of travelling so frequently, mostly for work but also for social purposes. "She's always going or coming!" remarks Rachel, shaking her head. "Sometimes I'm sure she is not aware of where exactly she is!"

Dependably late, the bus arrives and we pack Rachel and her baby onto it with hugs and snacks. I say my goodbyes to Charles and return to my hotel with nostalgia for my days in western Kenya and admiration for Rachel, who most certainly bounced her way west through the dark night on that decrepit Akamba bus clutching her nine-month-old son Valentine.

By now I've neglected my stomach to the point of being famished, as I do so often when travelling solo. I coax myself to the hotel's restaurant, where prices are higher than most nice places I would consider treating myself to back home. The buffet is the faster option, so I survey the spread and scoop a sample of one dish and another, trying to fill my plate with Kenyan food. I avoid the continental fare that never quite achieves tasty.

I hate eating alone and mostly bury my nose in that day's *Daily Nation*. When I do look up from the newspaper, my eyes are momentarily confused as they fall on a familiar face. It's Richard, the director of an NGO that fellow Canadians worked with in Nairobi while I was a volunteer in Ugunja so many years ago. During our short and unexpected reunion, Richard asks me eagerly about new funding opportunities for his work available through my agency. Who would be his best point of contact? Might they be interested in the new project he is proposing? While the shift in roles feels palpably odd, it feels good to share insider knowledge with this connection from my Kenyan past. Richard shakes my hand goodbye and returns to his party. My stomach churns. The random mix of food I've just shovelled back is sitting heavily in my bloated belly. On top of that, I'm struggling to digest my current reality.

I make myself a hot cup of tea back in room 348, which I notice is much more comfortable and full of amenities than the home I will return to tomorrow, than any home in Canada I am ever likely to return to. It's strange how comfort can be achieved through different means, sometimes material, sometimes not. My host family's kitchen, for example, a simple mud hut with a thatched roof on a small piece of land in rural western Kenya, used to feel like the cosiest spot in the evenings, the family and I gathered around the soft glow from a tin-can paraffin lamp, telling stories about our day.

I climb into bed and lean back against the soft pile of down pillows. I've brought an engaging book along for this business trip, which has involved my first visit to Tanzania, for meetings with some of our African partners, followed by a short week of working at our regional office in Nairobi. The book was penned by the late, great Polish foreign correspondent Ryszard Kapuściński. *Travels with Herodotus* was largely inspired by the author's absorption of the classic work he had toted along during his journeys—to India, to China, to Sudan, and farther afield. I have been enjoying the trusted company of his insights, and remind myself to recommend it to friends and colleagues whose minds are also intrigued by Earth's many places and cultures. At least I feel sure that the book will be worth the fines I'll owe when I return it late on Monday to the Ottawa Public Library. I sink back into his story and am soon moved to fold down the corner on page 79. On travel with Herodotus and Kapuściński alike, I have been dog-earing without restraint:

A journey, after all, neither begins in the instant we set out, nor ends when we have reached our doorstep once again. It starts much earlier and is really never over, because the film of memory continues running on inside of us long after we have come to a physical standstill. Indeed, there exists something like a contagion of travel, and the disease is essentially incurable.

I feel confronted with a particular album of that colourful film of memory from my previous stays in Kenya, and struck by the changed composition that would feature in images capturing this brief visit. Having graduated from being first a volunteer and then a student, I am now working for a Canadian donor agency and travelling in a completely different role. I have a suitcase instead of my backpack, and it is heavy not with hiking boots but with binders of background reading for our program meetings. This time I'm travelling in a different sphere of the country, yet acutely conscious of what lies beyond the privileged comfort of the luxury cars I've been shuttled around in, the multistar hotel I return to each evening, the professionals and executive directors whose company I keep. I can't shake knowing that the last time I was here, I stayed a five-minute walk away at the YMCA hostel, the cheapest safe lodging option near the city centre. I feel somehow estranged from my former intrepid self and ponder how I can be back in the country to which I have so often longed to return and yet so very far from the Kenya that I once knew and lived. My heart is conflicted as I assess if I have gone down the right path only to end up back in Kenya in such a different capacity.

By textbook standards, my career trajectory has been the model of incremental advance over the years. I started with a Canada World Youth exchange program; then, after completing a B.A. in international development (including a semester in Ghana), pursued a volunteer position in rural Kenya. I returned to Canada to do an M.A., carrying out my research in western Kenya. Finally, I secured an internship at a respected donor agency and months later landed a permanent position with its program on environment and African development that has afforded me the opportunity to return to Kenya. Reflecting on the evolution of my career somehow doesn't make me feel any better. I recall that I may have one more TUMS tablet floating somewhere in my zip-lock-bag pharmacy but manage to fall asleep before I bother to initiate the archaeological dig.

I spend my last day in Nairobi reconnecting with my friend Waswa, his spunky wife, Beryl, and their two energetic kids. Beryl and I talk about the American election while Waswa skilfully dodges *matatus* and meandering mutts on our drive to their home in Kibera. I comment on the (excessive?) scale of Kenyan jubilation following Obama's victory. The government of Kenya proclaimed a national holiday the day following the senator's win and Kenyans (especially the Luo tribe members) are eager to lay claim to the American president-elect. I have been contemplating the potential ramifications for Kenya of this new focus of (Western) worship, but Beryl puts it into perspective for me. She explains that Kenyans would be foolish to expect anything from Obama, and yet just as people feel proud and are moved to celebrate when their favourite football team secures a key victory, Kenyans are very reasonable to feel the excitement associated with Obama, who is clearly from their team. An historic victory on so many fronts within, but perhaps even more fascinatingly, beyond the United States. It occurs to me that the American dream just became global. Yes, we can.... That *we* has now been internalized by a population that cannot even fathom the reality of life for those born in the United States. Kenyans surely possess unwavering faith that Obama will not forget his past, will remember his Luo heritage as he leads his country ahead toward change.

Once we reach their home, Waswa and I catch up. It is easy to tell him about life in Canada, since he spent time working for Outward Bound in northern Ontario a few summers ago. He listens with a growing smile as I tell him about my September canoe trip on the Petawawa River. He laughs, remembering his experience learning to whitewater paddle, stuffing his lean body into a wetsuit to guard against the cold river.

After the brief afternoon visit, Waswa and Beryl drive me to the airport. We have to make a stop for gas along the way and then the car refuses to start again. Waswa recruits Beryl and me and the reluctant gas station attendant to roll start the car, and after a few failed attempts we manage to muscle the stubborn vehicle back into motion. I am secretly delighted that the car needed to be pushed and feel better now that my hands are dusty. I go after bidding goodbye and *kwa heri* to my friends and to Nairobi. My heart feels lighter after a brief but bright reconnection with this special family and their Kenya.

PETIT À PETIT, L'OISEAU FAIT SON NID

I try to settle in to absorb that I am leaving Kenya after having arrived only just a week ago. I'm sitting in the business-class section of the plane with more space than I feel comfortable having all to myself. My seatbelt is dutifully fastened and my oversized hand luggage jammed beneath the seat ahead of me for takeoff. I watch as the lights of Nairobi disappear behind us. I crane my neck, looking past the wings to follow as the glow fades into darkness while we speed ahead into the night.

We soar like a black kite, one of many birds my colleague pointed out when we visited Nairobi national park earlier in the week. The park is home to a number of winged types, including the darling yellow weaver birds, the males building a surplus of suspended nests to impress the ladies; the bushy-bodied ostrich haughtily parading across the grassy plains; the long-legged secretary bird sporting black knickers, extraordinary in all respects. Another African bird I've only seen depicted on fabric and ornamental crafts comes to mind. Sankofa is one of many Adinkra symbols I learned about when I was a student in Ghana. This mythic bird is depicted looking backward, with an egg representing the promise of the future in its mouth. Sankofa reminds us that sometimes we need to look back to be able to move forward.

I recall the first time I travelled to this continent, whose red soil left a permanent stain on my white running shoes. I was twenty years old when I went to Burkina Faso and grappled with everything foreign, sometimes wondering if I had landed on a different planet. One afternoon near the end of my three-month stay, my project leader, Andre, picked me up from my host family's compound. He waited by the tap in front of the house, where my young host sister, Salimata, collected a woman's coins and then strained her thin but wiry arms to help the stooped woman hoist the heavy bucket of water and balance it atop her head, a piece of fabric wound up like a donut to provide the slightest cushion between the hard metal and her tightly tressed hair. A splash of water sloshed over the edge of the bucket and refreshed a part of her dusty but colourful wrap skirt as the woman started her laboured walk back home.

I stretched my leg over the seat of the motorbike, waved to Salimata, and we were off. The village moved by at a pace I wasn't used to. It took on a different and more exciting dimension as we sped past family compounds, women selling savoury fried treats along the side of the road, a stall of brightly coloured flip-flops, small gangs of sheep. We toured about and then rode beyond the labyrinth of houses out to the *barrage*, where women were washing clothes. A large vegetable garden sprouted from the water's edge, where the job of irrigating during the dry season was made easier. Home a few weeks later, I would realize I didn't know the English word for *barrage*, or how to say *piler*, *diguet*, or *homologue* in my native tongue. I would feel a twinge of longing to be back in a place that I had felt vividly, but couldn't find the words to explain to family and friends eager to get a taste of my experiences in Africa.

Andre pulled up next to a small drinking spot and we were seated at a plastic table beneath the straw shade. We ordered cold drinks, which arrived warm. This rare one-on-one outing was my program leader's chance to debrief with me about my experience as a participant in the Canada World Youth exchange program. We chatted about the highs and lows of our group dynamics, of my relationship with Georgette, my Burkinabe counterpart. "Do you think the experience you've had here will influence what you choose to do next, Heidi?" he asked me. Not yet back in Canada and confronting the confusion of reintegration, I answered coolly in the negative.

"Non, pas trop." I wasn't sure. I figured I would return to university and pick up where I had left off after a first year of undergraduate studies in arts and sciences.

He reassured me by repeating a proverb he used often with our group, a call for patience when things were moving at a slower rate than we wanted: "Petit à petit, l'oiseau fait son nid." (Little by little the bird makes its nest.)

That Canada World Youth program—so many years ago now— had a remarkable impact on my life. Little did I know it as I naïvely sipped warm Coca-Cola from a dusty bottle in Djibo with Andre that day. That first exposure to Africa subtly but decidedly nudged the direction I have taken in my studies and travels since, and has influenced the career path I have pursued.

The wheels against the runway bring me back. I collect my things and shuffle off the plane for a short wait in Amsterdam. The layover is a phenomenon of stolen time, hours of freedom in a time zone and space continuum where I have no attachments, no responsibilities. I can float and explore—my identity, my tangled thoughts, the nearby city if time, courage, and currency affords. Airports remind me of the wide world that it is out there and the astounding diversity in shape, size, colour, language, and fashion that populates it. My sleep-starved mind starts to spin. I find a café and get a small, strong European coffee. The caffeine awakens the nagging internal questioning that has tagged along with me, my souvenir from Nairobi.

I feel decidedly unnerved by this trip. In contrast to other overseas adventures, this doesn't arise from the foreign nature of what I've seen or experienced but instead from how I've seen myself in a foreign way. The last time I was making my way home from Kenya, I was travelling with notebooks, cassette tapes, a laptop, and a mind all stuffed full of data collected for my master's degree research. My suitcases were laden with Christmas gifts from a good day's haggling at the Masai market. As a graduate student I had chosen to go back to Kenya to build on my volunteer experience at the UCRC and to take advantage of my social connections to facilitate my field research. That feeling of landing back in Ugunja, a community where I had lived, learned, and done my own laundry by hand, was like seeing a dear friend after years of separation. It was an assault of familiarity—sounds, smells, colours—but the passage of time was evident in little Nancy's legs, which now stretched taller, and in Aunt Angeline's forehead, now more deeply wrinkled. It felt wonderful to be back in that foreign familiar, and it took little time to find my flip-flop gait again. I loved returning to where so many walk on foot as they go to market, to school, to church, to work. And I loved feeling I had a reason to be there beyond aimless wandering and sightseeing. Conscious of the many corners of the world I had yet to discover, I relished having a reason to return to this place. My research afforded me the opportunity to meet a range of bright and passionate people, generous with their time and forthcoming about their experiences and opinions. While I had met equally interesting people on this work trip, I felt much less connected to the reality of Kenyan life during such a brief visit.

Stirred from my musing, I register that the loud speaker is inviting those bound for Ottawa to board the plane.

NO BEND, NO CURVE

The clock radio arrests my sleep. It hurts to be awake, and I feel emptied from the long flight back home to Ottawa. I reach to mute the radio's din but then register that the woman's voice is listing names—Alpha Yaya Diallo, Madagascar Slim, Kofi Ackah—and talking about highlife, Afropop, soukous and other musical genres that these African immigrants to Canada have continued to create. She plays a bright track with Cameroonian guitar and I feel the rhythm in my feet, a memory of movement so familiar. I am immediately awake enough to feel nostalgic for the humid Wednesday night concerts held at the Alliance Française in Accra. Given that this venue was just down the road from the university, (straight straight, no bend, no curve—the specific directions supplied), it was an easy expedition from Legon campus, where I had elected to complete my final semester of undergraduate studies at the University of Ghana.

Other, more far-flung destinations were less straightforward to reach in Ghana and I quickly learned the necessity of asking directions. Despite arming myself with maps, street names, and my best effort to be self-sufficient, I soon realized that the only way to navigate the country was to ask for help, again and again. With a little *me-pa-wo-cho* (literally "I beg of you," the way to say "please" in Twi), a lot of *meh-daa-se-paa* (thank you), and the generous patience of so many approachable Ghanaians, I was lucky to see a lot of the country. Perhaps it is no coincidence that the Twi words that are still retrievable after so many years and layers of other accumulated foreign vocabulary are directional. I can hear my gregarious language teacher, Kofi, leading us in a choral recitation of *faa benkum, faa nifa, faa wanim teeee, faa wanim teeee* (go left, go right, go straight ahead, go straight ahead). At the end of each class, he sent us away with our tongues tired of Twi twisting, telling us *Ko bra* (You go and come). This expression has forever amused me, unanchored as it is to any particular timeframe. You could be expected to go and come in five minutes or in five years, the time horizon never explicitly indicated by the speaker. It also comforted me to hear this phrase when I said goodbye to my Ghanaian friend and classmate Yvonne at the end of my stay.

"You go and come," she said and helped me pile my bags into the taxi bound for the airport.

Beyond learning to ask for directions in Ghana, I also learned that my Western linear logic was not always compatible with West African reality.

LONELY PLANET, WEST AFRICA

Who would miss the chance to arrive or leave Ada Foah by river ferry?
—*Lonely Planet* guidebook

With one week remaining in Ghana and no particular plan, my American roommate and I decided to go on one last adventure—to Togo. The idea was to pursue a transportation combination, take the ferry from Ada Foah up the Volta River to Kpong, continue east by road to Ho, and then across the border to Kpalime in Togo. After procuring our visas, packing our small bags with sun-faded clothes, and making our way through the frenetic city, with its constant soundtrack of car horns and street hawkers, we were directed to the mini-bus heading to Ada Foah.

On checking in at Cokoloko, the modest beach hotel in Adah Foah that our friends had recommended, we were informed that the ferry "was finished." Much to our dismay, it had recently ceased to offer passage up the river. By now resilient to changes in plans, we decided to take advantage of the beach and hammocks and set out by road for Ho early the next morning.

Quite different from our planned scenic cruise, the next day found us on a *tro-tro* riding spree thanks to our attachment to a linear model of logic. Instead of going the circuitous way we were being advised (backtrack west to Accra, catch a bus all the way east to Aflao, and then go northwest to Ho) we saw the straight and direct line connecting the dots between Ada Foah and a string of small villages on our map as a much more logical route. What we experienced, however, was an uncomfortable, slow, and painful trajectory. We rode in the M*A*S*H-style trucks that made us feel like soldiers going off to war. Lots of laughing and a little dozing off were all we could do to distract our limbs and extremities from their immense displeasure. At one point, the ladies on board the *tro-tro* to Adidome starting zealously yelling "Ho! Ho! Ho!" out of the window to attract the attention of a passing vehicle. The car stopped and took all of us going to Ho with it. The ladies had saved us a long roadside wait, their Santa Claus call answering our holiday travel wish.

DISCONNECTED

The upbeat melodies emanating from my radio move me to crawl out from under my warm blankets. The music has triggered a flow of memories and I find myself thinking about my dear friend Rose, whom I was not able to connect with during this short business trip to Nairobi. It occurs to me that on a normal day, the memories of my experiences in Africa are like a magic genie trapped in a bottle. The genie is rarely coaxed out into my day-to-day Ontario existence. But as soon as I hit African soil, I am often overwhelmed by a deluge of recollections.

I once spent an almost sleepless night in a youth hostel in Nairobi. It was during my first trip to Kenya, and the night I arrived found me confused as I lay shivering with cold after leaving a sweaty Toronto September behind for the tropics. I felt entranced by a dizzying flood of memories of my past experiences in West Africa. I frantically searched the corners of my mind for the names of various residences and halls on the University of Ghana campus: Akuafo Hall, where we ate lunch; Mensah Saba, where my friend Yvonne lived; the illustrious girls-only residence, Volta Hall; the ruckus of the boys' Commonwealth Hall. I felt an urgent need to reconnect with these words. I had visions of places I'd visited and people I'd met whom I hadn't thought of for years. In that moment, I felt keenly aware that an important and formative part of my lived experience lay dormant and as distant from my calm Canadian life as the turbulent continent itself. Little at home triggered these memories. Of course, I would go through the period of enlightenment when I came home and be inspired to read books on African politics and history and to maintain correspondence with my new friends, but after some time, I would return to Ondaatje and Atwood, abandon highlife for the latest indie hits, and drift back to preoccupations that were easier to share with my Canadian friends. From time to time, I would have a reason to tell a story of my African adventures, but it was never very satisfying, never easy to communicate in a way that felt I was doing justice to the richness of my experience, to the people who taught me so much. Moving from one apartment to the next over the years, the colourful fabrics and wood carvings so carefully selected during my travels were mostly packed into boxes, waiting until I settled into a home of my own.

I decide to call my Kenyan friend Rose to catch up since we hadn't been able to see each other while I was in Nairobi. Though we hail from totally different cultures and sides of the world, we developed a close connection soon after we met. We shared a common sense of humour, developed a number of inside jokes, and spent a lot of time together. For no reason in particular, I feel nervous as the phone rings. She answers with a loud hello. She is in Mombasa for a meeting with some people from Microsoft. She is at a restaurant watching a premier league football game and has just enjoyed *ugali* and fish for dinner. Her brother Ford and cousin Madhiaba are home for a visit. I tell myself to remember to send them something thoughtful, perhaps a magazine about football? The line is fuzzy and the noise from the TV in the background is loud and distracting. I tell Rose, "I don't really have anything to say ... " and she laughs at my joke, this line used as the opening to many long-winded speeches we have both endured at conferences and meetings together in Kenya. She sends sunshine and warmth to the family here in Canada. She asks me when I'm coming to Kenya again. I laugh. "I've just arrived home! Let me remember how to be a Canadian for a bit, Rose," I say, only slightly joking.

"How did it feel to be home?" Rose asks me. I hesitate for a moment, trying to determine where she is speaking about. Realizing she is referring to Kenya, I tell her it felt too squeezed. I tell her about having to visit Rachel and Charles at the Akamba station. "Come on!" She says. "You mean...."

"Seriously!" I say, laughing.

"Oh ... sorry!" she apologizes. "Really, you have come and gone too quick," she says. She presses to know when I might have an occasion to travel again to Kenya. I tell her about a conference planned for the spring that I may be able to convince my boss I should attend. But I'm not certain we'll be attending the event or that I would even have time to make the journey to Ugunja.

I try to tell her about the struggle I had being back in Kenya this time. I talk about how strange I felt staying at the fancy hotel in Nairobi and riding taxis instead of *matatus*. She congratulates me for moving up in the world and suggests I hang on tight to my job, especially if it affords me the chance to travel frequently to Kenya. I try to make her understand, and go on about how I felt like a serious *muzungu* (foreigner), staying at such an expensive hotel when I know there are so many going without even the most meagre shelter in Nairobi's crowded slums. I try not to sound ungrateful.

"It would have been much nicer to stay at home with you and Aunt Angeline in Ugunja," I tell her.

"Of course—east, west, home is best!" She chants this familiar rhyme that so many of my Luo friends have repeated to me. "But tell me, how is the new job?" she asks with curiosity. I pause, searching for words. I start to describe some of the challenges I have with my new position, but the call gets interrupted.

The line is breaking up. We are cut off, abruptly disconnected. I think about calling back but hesitate. It is hard to understand her with static muffling the line. It is also difficult to find common ground, to know what to talk about. My stories feel trivial. I think about sending an email, or writing a letter like I used to do before they had an internet connection in Ugunja. I think maybe things will be clearer if I put them into words, if I express them through writing.

I sit down and pick up a pen. . . .

Notes and Acknowledgments

INTRODUCTION

1 *Canadian Encyclopedia*, s.v. "Colombo Plan," http://thecanadianencyclopedia. com/index.cfm?PgNm=TCE&Params=A1ARTA0001771 (accessed August 20, 2010).

2 Paolo Freire, *Pedagogy of the Oppressed*, 30th anniversary ed., trans. Myra Bergman Ramos (New York: Continuum, 2000).

3 Amartya Sen, *Development as Freedom* (Oxford: Oxford University Press, 1999).

4 GNI differs from GDP (gross domestic product) in that it includes inter-country income transfers, in effect attributing to a territory the product generated within it as well as the incomes received in it. GNI is becoming the standard national economic indicator. Organisation for Economic Co-operation and Development, StatExtracts, ODA by Donor, "Development," http://stats.oecd.org/Index.aspx?DataSetCode=ODA_DONOR (accessed August 8, 2010).

5 Jennifer Paul and Marcus Pistor, *Official Development Assistance Spending*, Parliamentary Information and Research Service, revised 13 May 2009, http://www2.parl.gc.ca/Content/LOP/ResearchPublications/ prb0710-e.pdf, 2.

6 UNICEF, *0.7% Background*, May 22, 2007, http://www.unicef.ca/portal/ Secure/Community/502/WCM/HELP/take_action/G8/Point7_EN2.pdf; Organisation for Economic Co-operation and Development, *Development Aid at Its Highest Level Ever in 2008*, 30 March 2009, http://www.oecd.org/ dataoecd/47/52/42458612.pdf, Chart 1: DAC Members' Net Official Development Assistance in 2008.

7 Paul and Pistor, *Official Development Assistance Spending*, 2.

8 Andrew Woodcock, "Britain Tops G8 Nations in Overseas Aid Says Report," *The Independent*, June 21, 2010, http://www.independent.co.uk/news/uk/politics/britain-tops-g8-nations-in-overseas-aid-says-report-2006630.html (accessed August 7, 2010).

9 Thomson Reuters Foundation, AlertNet, Fact Sheet: How Does Food Aid Work? http://www.alertnet.org/thefacts/reliefresources/11268811061.htm (accessed July 8, 2010).

10 Stephen Brown, "Aid Effectiveness and the Framing of New Canadian Aid Initiatives," in *Readings in Canadian Foreign Policy: Classic Debates and New Ideas*, 2nd ed., ed. Duane Bratt and Christopher J. Kukucha (Toronto: Oxford University Press, 2011, 472).

11 *Ibid.*

12 Standing Senate Committee on Foreign Affairs and International Trade, *Overcoming 40 Years of Failure: A New Road Map for sub-Saharan Africa*, February 2007, http://www.parl.gc.ca/39/1/parlbus/commbus/senate/com-e/fore-e/rep-e/repafrifeb07-e.pdf.

13 Nilima Gulrajani, "How Politicization Has Been Silently Killing CIDA's Effectiveness," *Globe and Mail*, June 5, 2009, http://www.theglobeandmail.com/news/opinions/how-politicization-has-been-silently-killing-cidas-effectiveness/article1171666 (accessed July 8, 2010).

14 Office of the Auditor General, *Strengthening Aid Effectiveness: Canadian International Development Agency*, Report to the House of Commons, Fall 2009, ch. 8, www.oag-bvg.gc.ca/internet/English/parl_oag_200911_08_e_33209.html (accessed August 8, 2010).

15 Stockholm International Peace Research Institute, SIPRI Military Expenditure Database, "Canada," http://milexdata.sipri.org/result.php4 (accessed December 5, 2010).

16 Canada, Cabinet Committee on Afghanistan, *Canada's Engagement in Afghanistan*, Report to Parliament, December 2008, http://www.afghanistan.gc.ca/canada-afghanistan/documents/r02_09/aid.aspx?lang=en (accessed November 7, 2010).

17 Alistair Leithead, "Inside Kandahar's Casualty," BBC News, January 21, 2009, http://news.bbc.co.uk/2/hi/programmes/newsnight/7842857.stm (accessed November 7, 2010); Wayne Kondro, "Troubled Afghan Hospital Needs Canadian SWAT Team," *Canadian Medical Association Journal* 177, no. 8 (October 9, 2007): 837–39.

18 Canadian Council for International Co-operation, *Canada's 3D Approach*, Presentation to the Standing Committee on Defence and Veteran Affairs, Ottawa, November 2005, http://www.ccic.ca/what_we_do/policy_international_e.php

(accessed November 26, 2010); Patrick Travers and Taylor Owen, *Peacebuilding While Peacemaking: The Merits of a 3D Approach in Afghanistan*, http://cicam.ruhosting.nl/teksten/act.07.grotenhuis.owen%20paper.pdf.

19 Brown, "Aid Effectiveness," 473–74; Julian Wright, *Canada in Afghanistan: Assessing the 3-D Approach* (Waterloo, ON: Institute for Research on Public Policy, 2005).

20 United Nations Association in Canada, *Canada and UN Peacekeeping*, http://www.unac.org/peacekeeping/en/un-peacekeeping/fact-sheets/canada-and-un-peacekeeping (accessed August 7, 2010).

21 *Ibid*.

22 Foreign Affairs and International Trade Canada, *Canada in the North Atlantic Treaty Organization (NATO)*, http://www.international.gc.ca/nato-otan/canada.aspx (accessed August 7, 2010).

23 Geoffrey York, "Banned Aid," *Globe and Mail*, May 29, 2009, http://www.theglobeandmail.com/news/opinions/banned-aid/article1160311 (accessed July 8, 2010).

24 Yves Engler, *The Black Book of Canadian Foreign Policy* (Black Point, NS: Fernwood Publishing/RED Publishing, 2009), 31–33.

25 The Interim Cooperation Framework was set up after the 2004 coup to form the basis of a national development program covering Haiti's needs in the short and medium term. Members of the ICF included influential donor countries, the European Commission and the European Union, and international financial institutions such as the World Bank and the Inter-American Development Bank. Richard Saunders, "Helping the Neo-Liberal Destruction of Haiti's Economy: Haiti's Civil Society Denounced the ICF," *Press for Conversion!* 60 (March 2007): 23.

26 Engler, *Black Book*, 31; Stephen Kerr, "Gildan's Haitian Sweatshops," *Press for Conversion!* 60 (March 2007): 44.

27 Beverly Bell, "Foreign-led Commission Now Runs Haiti," *Truthout*, May 16, 2010, http://www.truthout.org/foreign-led-commission-now-governs-haiti59537 (accessed August 7, 2010).

28 *Ibid*.

29 Anthony Fenton, "Haiti: Private Contactors Like Vultures Coming to Grab the Loot," *Global Research*, February 21, 2010, http://www.globalresearch.ca/index.php?context=va&aid=17731 (accessed August 27, 2010).

30 Canada Haiti Action Network News Service, "Ottawa Spending Earthquake Funds on Building Jails and Equipping Police," May 9, 2010, http://canadahaitiaction.ca/node/341 (accessed November 5, 2010); CTV News, "Amid Hurricane Threat, Canada Pledges Haitian Aid," November 4,

2010, http://news.sympatico.ctv.ca/canada/cannon_promised_more_support_for_haiti_as_storm_looms/e50d7876 (accessed November 5, 2010).

31 Shawn McCarthy, "Canada, a Quiet Powerhouse in Africa's Mining Sector," *Globe and Mail*, May 10, 2010, http://www.theglobeandmail.com/news/world/g8-g20/africa/canada-a-quiet-powerhouse-in-africas-mining-sector/article1562696/?cid=art-rail-g20africa (accessed July 8, 2010).

32 *Ibid.*

33 *Ibid.*; Engler, *Black Book*, 175–79.

34 Canadian Council for International Co-operation, *Africa Matters: Time for a Renewed Commitment to Economic and Social Justice for Africa*, Africa–Canada Forum Backgrounder, 2010, http://www.ccic.ca/_files/en/working_groups/acf_2010-04_africa_matters_backgrounder_e.pdf.

35 York, "Banned Aid."

36 *Ibid.*

37 Joanna Smith, "Canada to Double Aid to Africa," *The Star*, May 23, 2009, http://www.thestar.com/News/Canada/article/607147 (accessed July 8, 2010).

38 CBC News, "No Abortion in Canada's G8 Maternal Health Plan," April 26, 2010, http://www.cbc.ca/politics/story/2010/04/26/abortion-maternal-health.html (accessed August 7, 2010).

39 TheSpec.com, "Aid Groups Suffering from 'Abortion Chill,'" May 16, 2010, http://www.thespec.com/article/770379 (accessed August 7, 2010).

40 An open letter to Stephen Harper developed by ACPD and the Adhoc Coalition for Women's Equality and Human Rights, May 14, 2010, http://mdg5at10.org/index.php?option=com_content&view=article&id=28:an-open-letter-to-stephen-harper-developed-by-acpd-and-the-adhoc-coalition-for-womens-equality-and-human-rights&catid=1:latest-news&Itemid=2 (accessed November 6, 2010).

41 Canadian Council for International Co-operation, "CIDA Funding to CCIC Threatened: Canada's Foreign Aid Community Risks Losing Strong Voice for the World's Poor," news release, June 1, 2010, http://www.ccic.ca/_files/en/media/news_2010-06_01_ccic_funding.pdf; Canadian Council for International Cooperation, *De-funding Backgrounder*, June 2010, http://www.ccic.ca/_files/en/media/backgrounder_defunding_e.pdf.

42 John Ivison, "Funding for Leftist Group to Be Cut," *National Post*, December 5, 2009, http://www.nationalpost.com/opinion/columnists/story.html?id=2e5f8e01-984e-4b95-91a3-f0a50a4afee8 (accessed October 4, 2010).

43 CBC News, "Rights and Democracy Torn by Dissent," February 4, 2010, http://www.cbc.ca/canada/story/2010/02/03/rights-democracy-dissent.html

(accessed August 7, 2010); Safia Lakhani and Alexandra Dodger, "Rights and Democracy Undermined by Feds: Ideology Should Not Motivate Funding Allocations," *The McGill Daily*, February 18, 2010, http://www.mcgilldaily.com/articles/26928 (accessed August 7, 2010).

44 Chimamanda Adichie, "The Danger of a Single Story," TED video, 18:49, filmed July 2009, posted October 2009, http://www.ted.com/talks/chimamanda_adichie_the_danger_of_a_single_story.html (accessed July 8, 2010).

45 Chinua Achebe, *Home and Exile* (New York: Oxford University Press, 1998), 79; Adichie, "The Danger of a Single Story."

46 Richard Day, quoted in Nicholas Klassen, "Escape 'Work,' Get a Life: Interview with Richard Day" in *Geez* 17 (Spring 2010), 36–40.

CHAPTER 5

For everything that I was able to understand about displacement as daily life, I am indebted to all those who lent me such a prodigious degree of trust. This work is dedicated to each of you. I regret that the sincerity of my gratitude cannot translate into a more secure future for anyone who believed it would.

1 Shan Human Rights Foundation and the Shan Women's Action Network, *License to Rape* (Chiang Mai, Thailand: The Foundation, 2002).

2 Dr. Sein Win, Prime Minister in Exile, "Burma: Current Situation, Future Prospects," Keynote speech at a human rights conference organized by the Burma Solidarity Collective and the McGill Human Rights Working Group, McGill University, Montreal, November 29, 2004.

3 The State Peace and Development Council (SPDC) is the name of Burma's military dictatorship.

CHAPTER 7

1 Several reviewers have pointed out that using the term "black Africa" sounds archaic, colonialist, and, by extension, racist. I do realize this, though have preferred to retain it for two reasons. First, I wanted to distinguish between the sub-Saharan region and North Africa. Though I haven't yet been to the region, I believe an immersion in North Africa would be less of a shock (for me, at least), given my Middle Eastern colouring. I just wouldn't stick out as much. Second, and more subtly, when I wrote the passage I thought (and still think) that I was doing something fundamentally colonialist, and I wanted to evoke those feelings with my language. I wanted to shock and to cause some debate, which has already happened among my friends and family. Any offence caused is my responsibility and not the editors'.

2 Although some writing systems are indigenous to Africa, it is most likely that the writing of Kinyarwanda began with Latin script used by Christian missionaries in the late nineteenth and early twentieth centuries during German and Belgium colonization.

Contributors

Maro Adjemian has a B.Sc. in biology with a minor in international development studies and an M.A. in geography, both from McGill University. She lives in Montreal and teaches at Vanier College, focusing on international environmental and social justice issues. She is also on the board of directors of Association Burkina Canada, an NGO that sponsors the education of orphans in Burkina Faso.

Alisha Nicole Apale has a B.A. in the social studies of medicine and an M.Sc. in international health. She currently works in Ottawa in Aboriginal maternal and child health. Her interest in development is centred on global health and is shaped by the deeply instructive experiences of studying, living, and working in Thailand, India, Kenya, and several European Union countries. She is particularly focused on health and illness as experienced by vulnerable populations within highly inequitable countries, including Canada.

Heidi Braun works at the International Development Research Centre in Ottawa. Her job takes her to Africa every six months and she always makes sure to get out of the hotel.

Alika Hendricks works as a lawyer for Legal Aid Ontario and volunteers with Peacebuilders International to help criminally involved youth tap into supportive networks and make better choices. She hopes to develop practical skills to effect positive change in communities both at home and overseas.

Zoe Kahn returned to Canada after completing graduate studies in the United Kingdom and joined the federal government in 2006, where she has since worked on a range of domestic and international social policy issues. In 2010, Zoe completed a year's CIDA posting to Afghanistan, serving as the development advisor to Task Force Kandahar.

Pike Krpan is an international development studies graduate. She has worked for PEN Canada, *Descant*, and *Shameless* magazine and currently works as a freelance writer and editor. Her current passions are anti-racist, queer, and sex worker rights community organizing in Toronto.

Julia Paulson travels regularly to Peru, where she conducted her doctoral research. She lives in the United Kingdom, where she is completing a Ph.D. in education.

Laura Madeleine Sie completed her B.Sc. and M.Sc. in aerospace and mechanical engineering, respectively, in pursuit of her childhood dream of becoming an astronaut. However, a six-month placement in Kenya awakened her passion for international development and altered her career path. Her current work involves HIV prevention in southern Africa.

Valerie Stam is a community developer at a community health centre in Ottawa, where she enjoys translating her overseas development experience into local practice. Since travelling to Cameroon at the age of fifteen, Valerie's views on development continue to be shaped by her experiences. Over the years she has studied income generation among refugees in Ghana, researched the women's peace movement in Senegal, and explored the intersection of women, politics, and conflict in India.

Simon Strauss is an environmental consultant in Toronto. He has worked at two firms during his three-plus years in the field, compiling environmental assessments for nuclear, mining, and waterfront developments. His experiences abroad have taught him the importance of taking setbacks in stride, keeping a sense of humour about work and life, and talking with as many people as possible to get the inside scoop on how things work.